The Analog
Gothique Blend

The Analog
Gothique Blend

Published by
The Wapshott Press, LLC
PO Box 31513
Los Angeles, CA 90031
www.WapshottPress.com

Copyright © 2014 Tom Good

First printing November 2014

All rights reserved. No part of this is publication may be reproduced or transmitted in any form or by any means, electronic or mechanical, including photocopy, recording, or any information storage and retrieval system now known or to be invented, without permission in writing from the publisher, except by a reviewer who wishes to quote brief passages in connection with a review written for inclusion in a magazine, newspaper, or broadcast.

ISBN: 978-1-942007-00-5

06 05 04 03 4 3 2 1

Edited by Cristina Coppinger
Cover design by Thomas Good
Book design by Ginger Mayerson

The Analog

Gothique Circus Cabaret. Created by Lisa Rife aka Gothique Smooch.
A community / family of circus, burlesque, sideshow artists and performers.

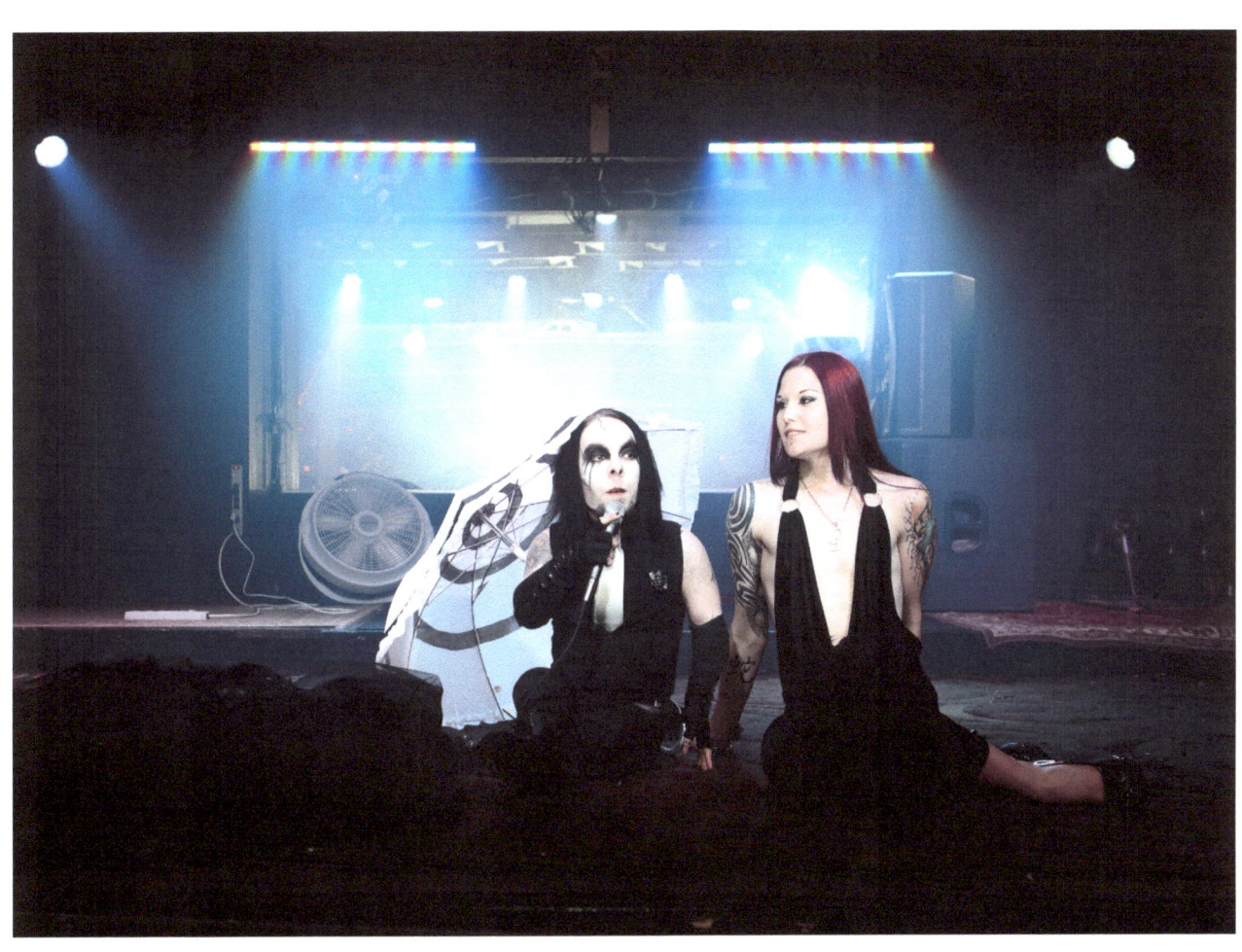

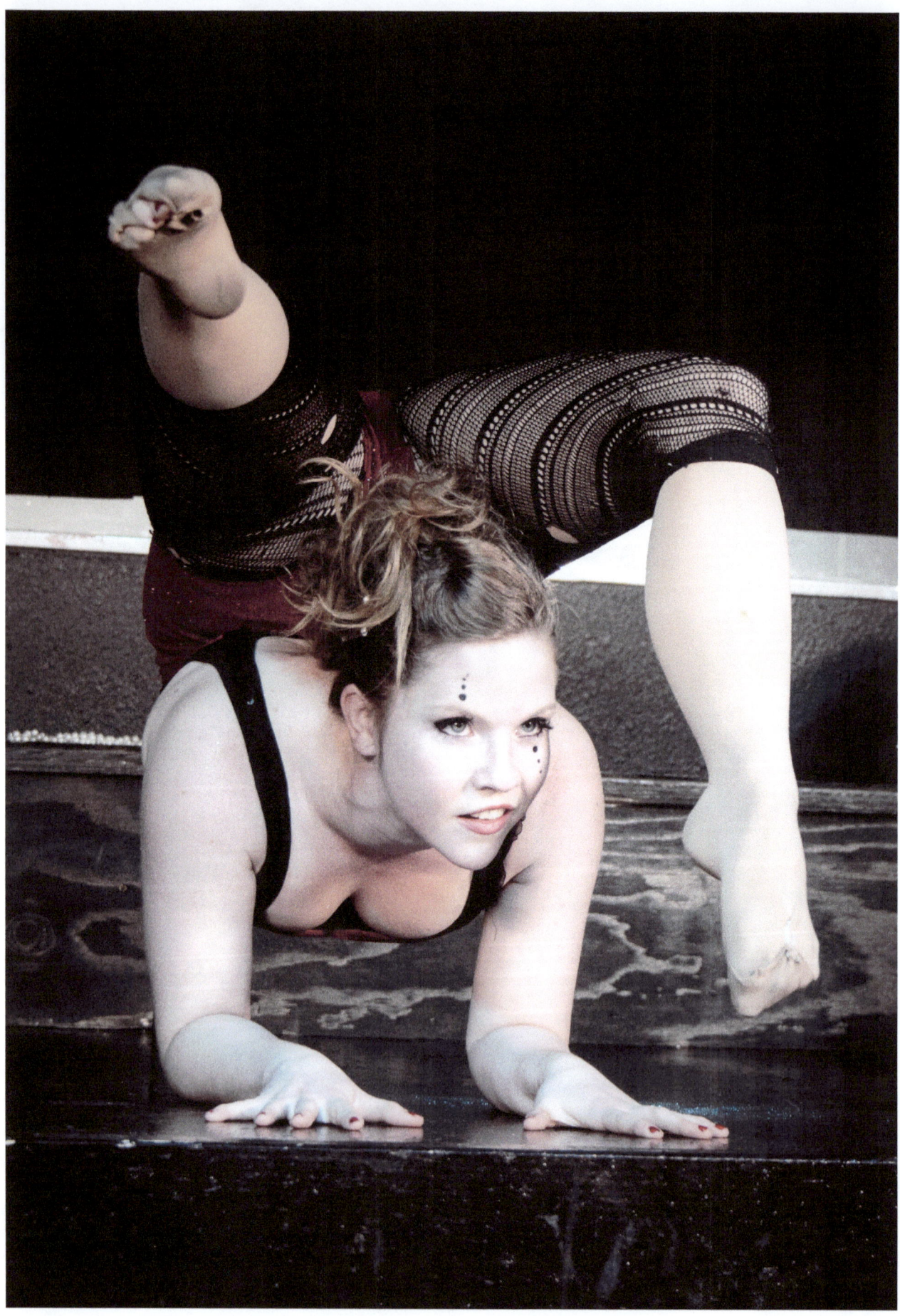

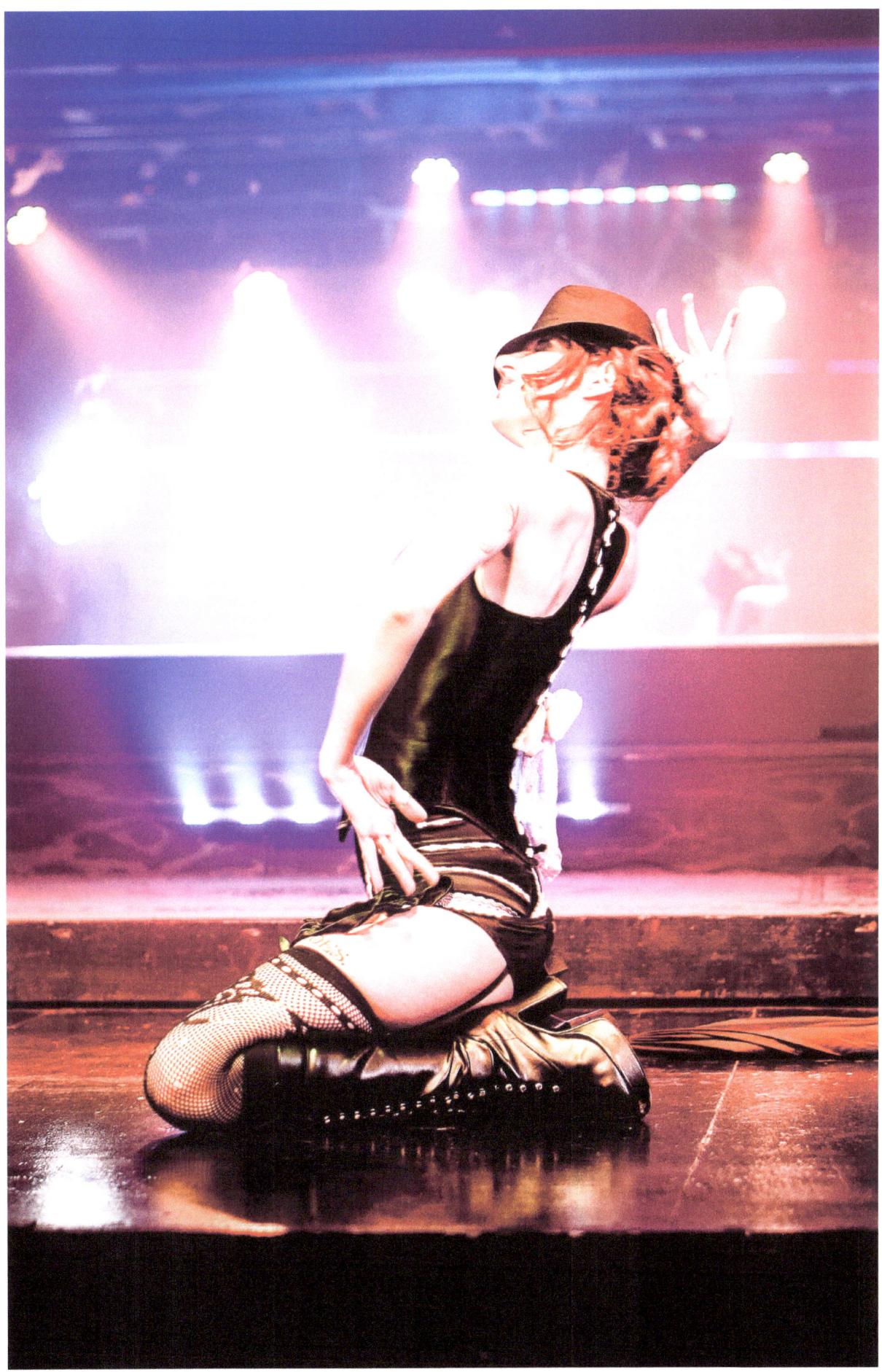

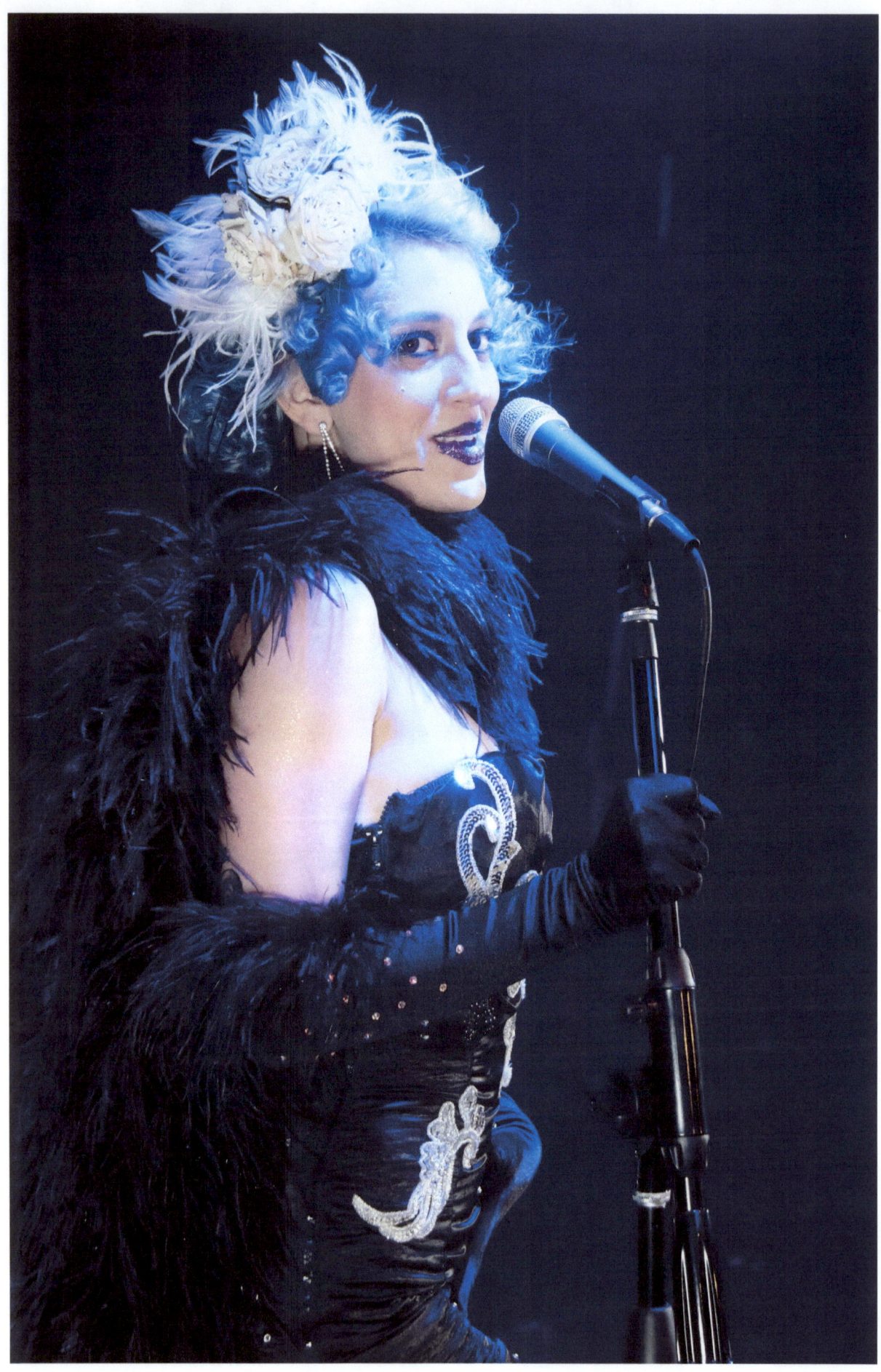

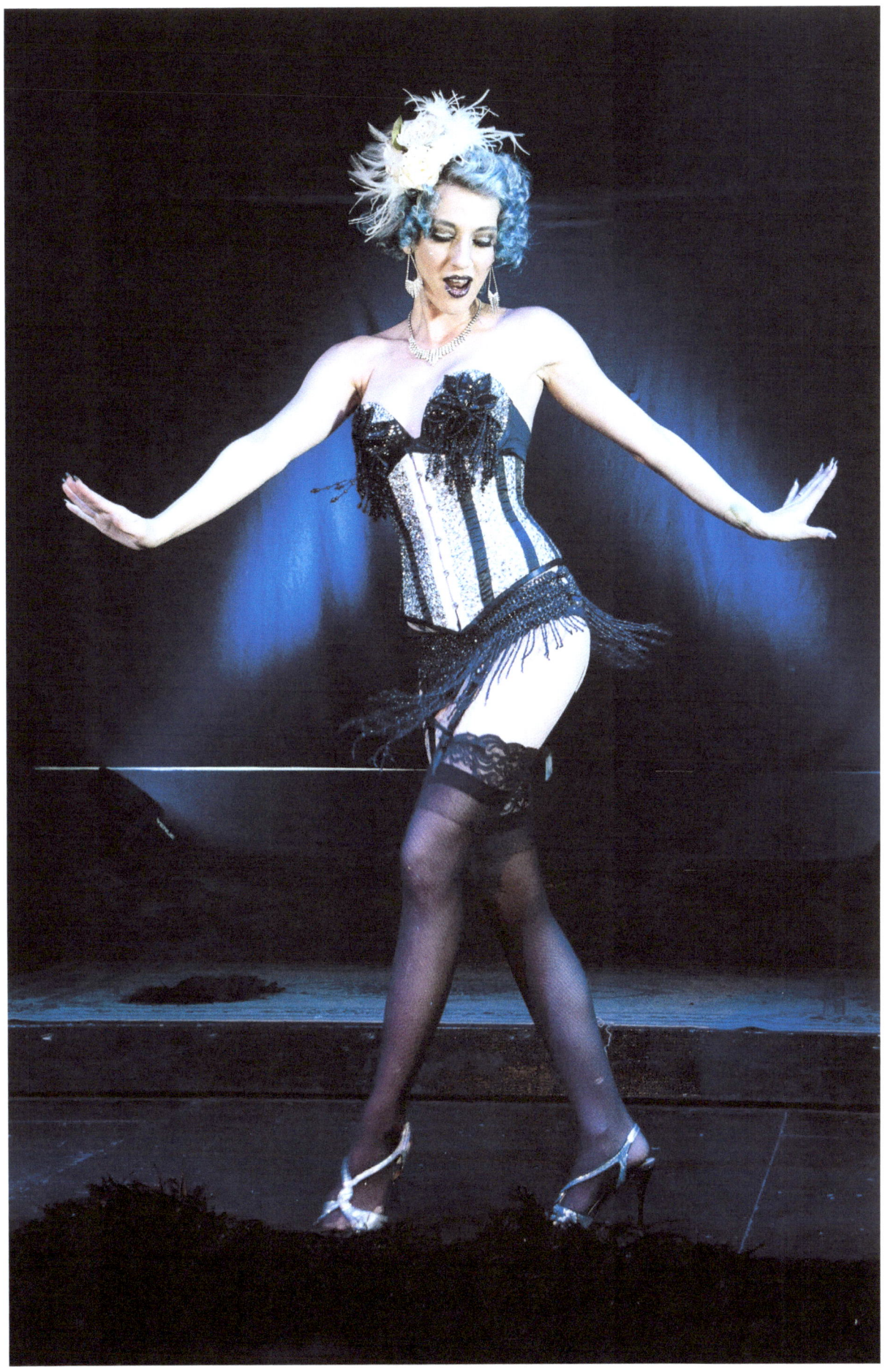

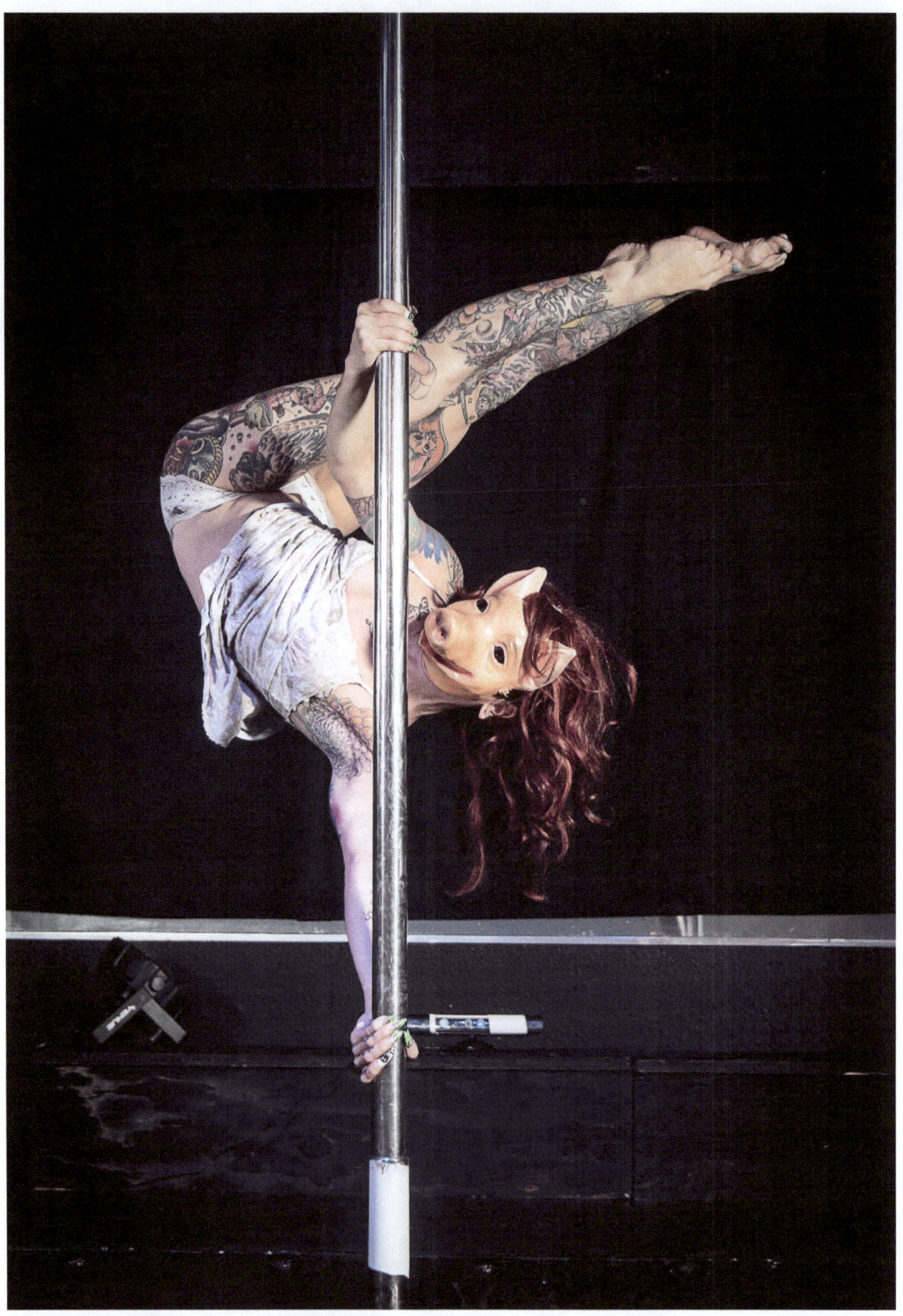

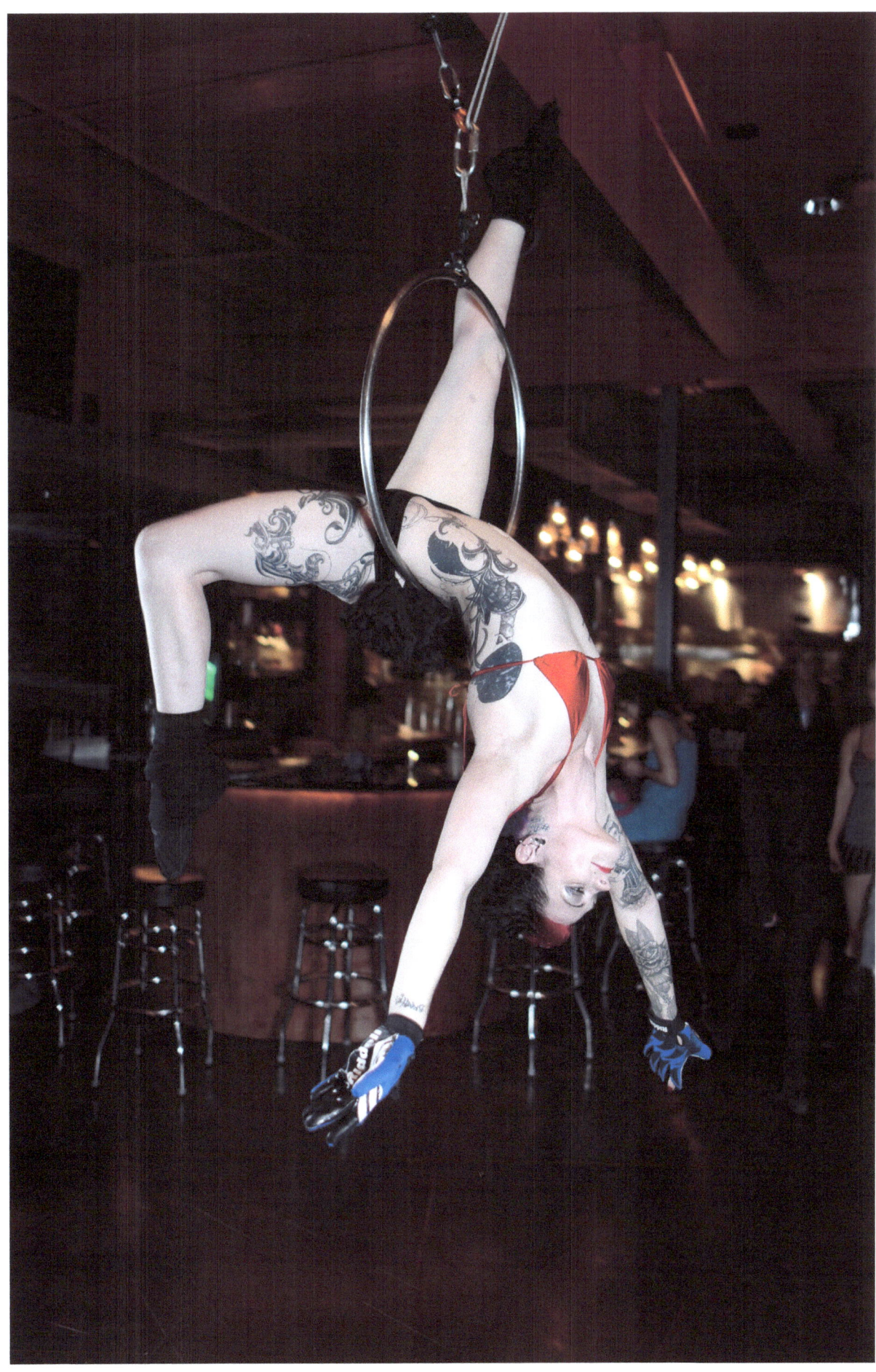

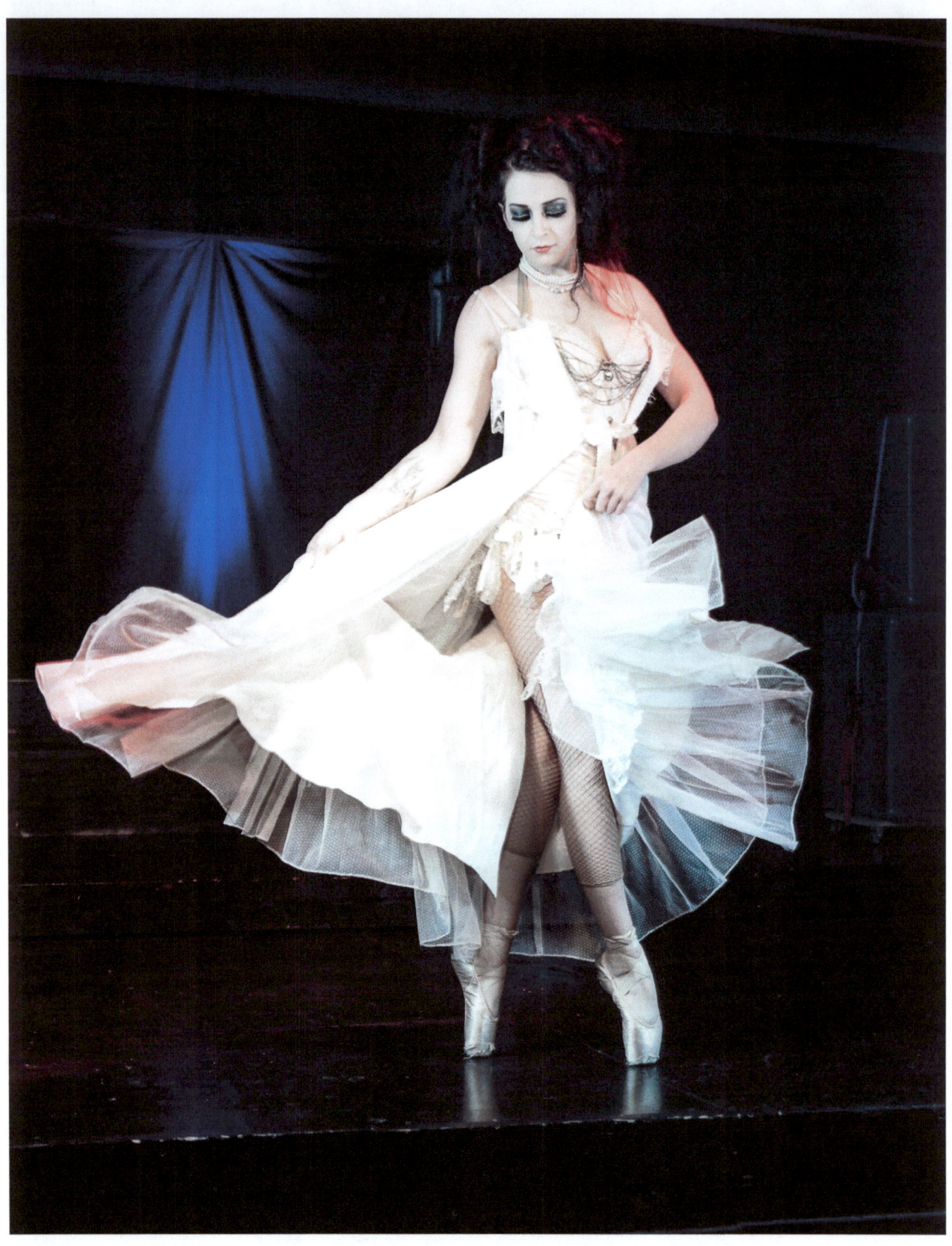

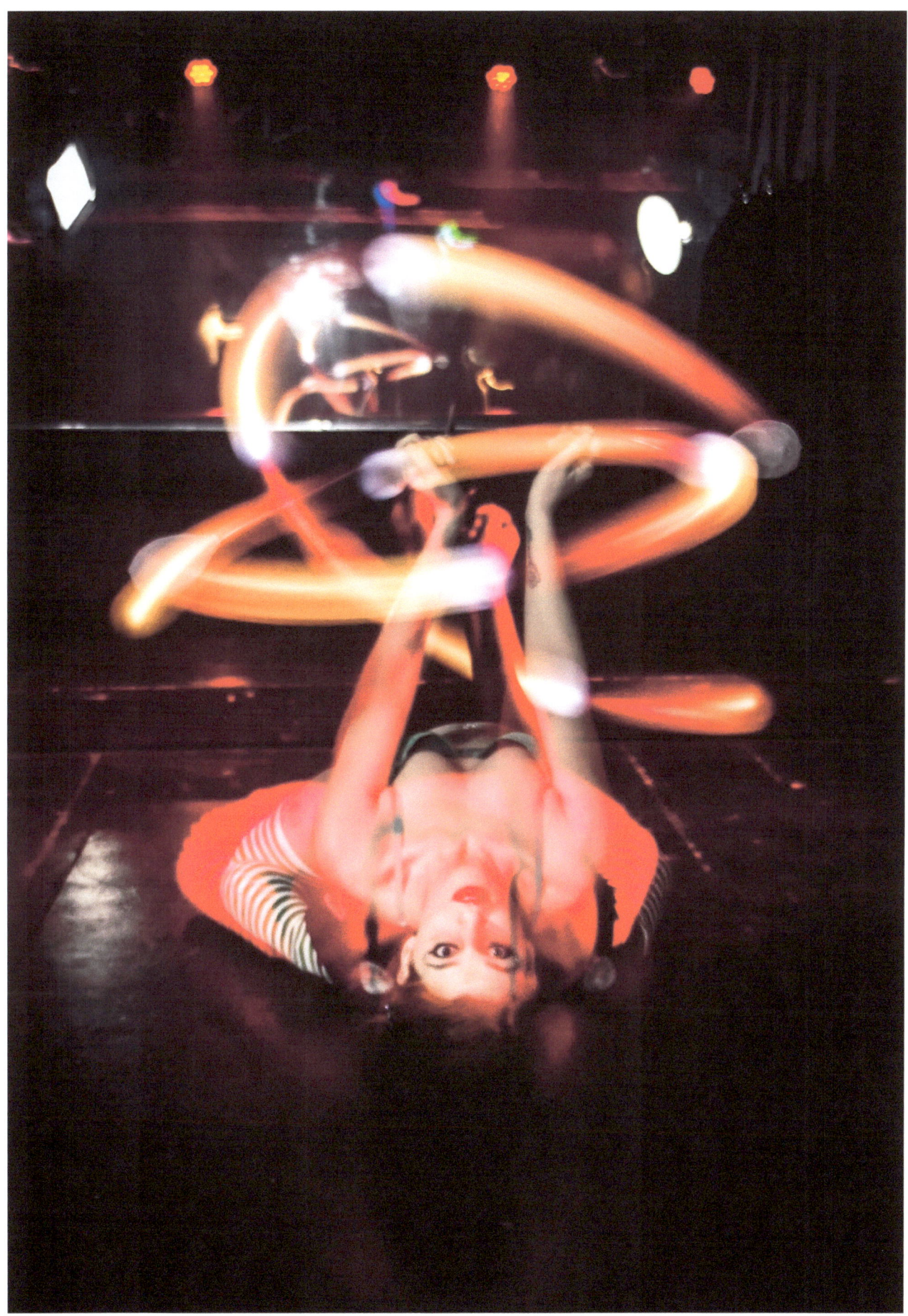

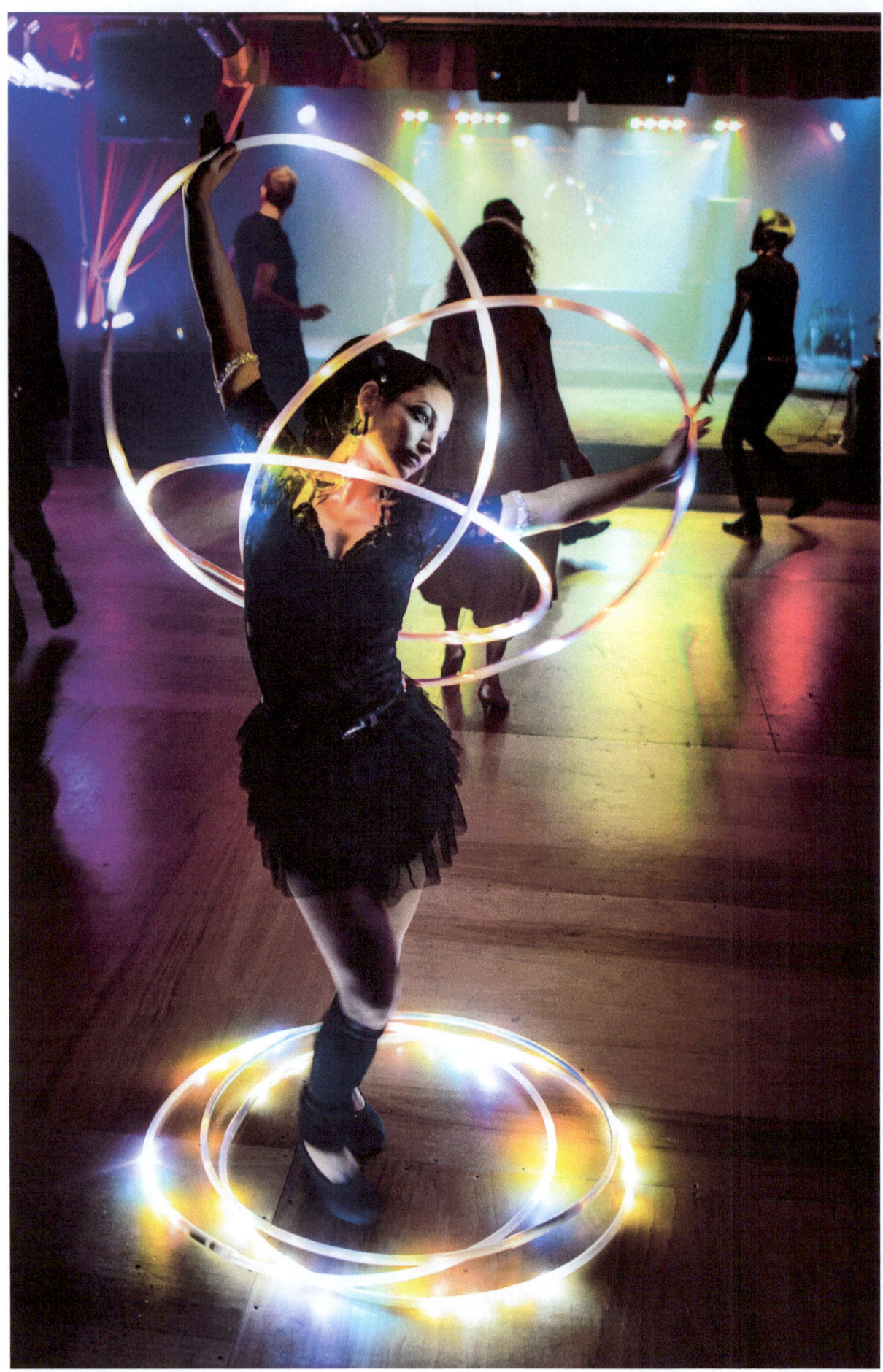

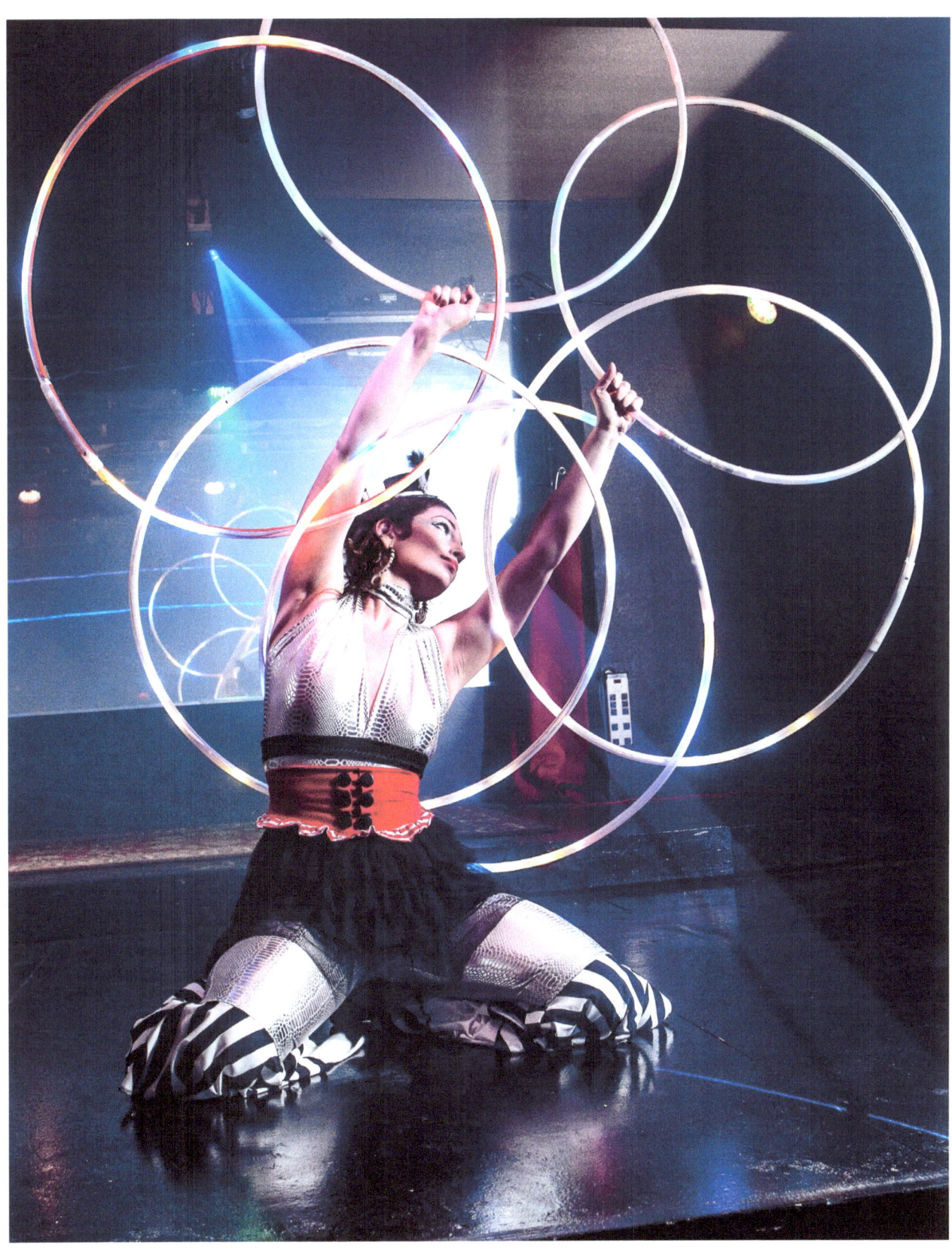

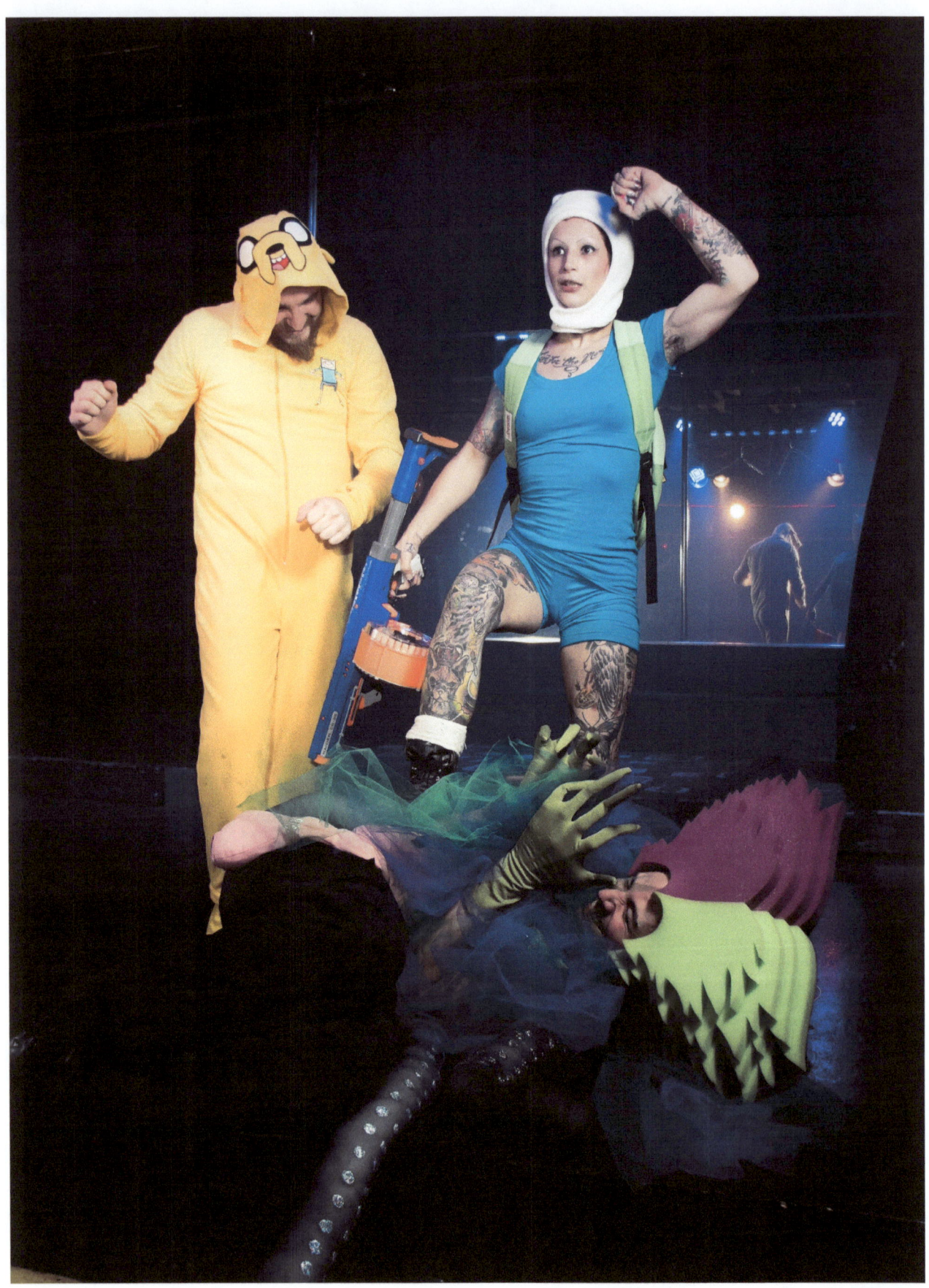

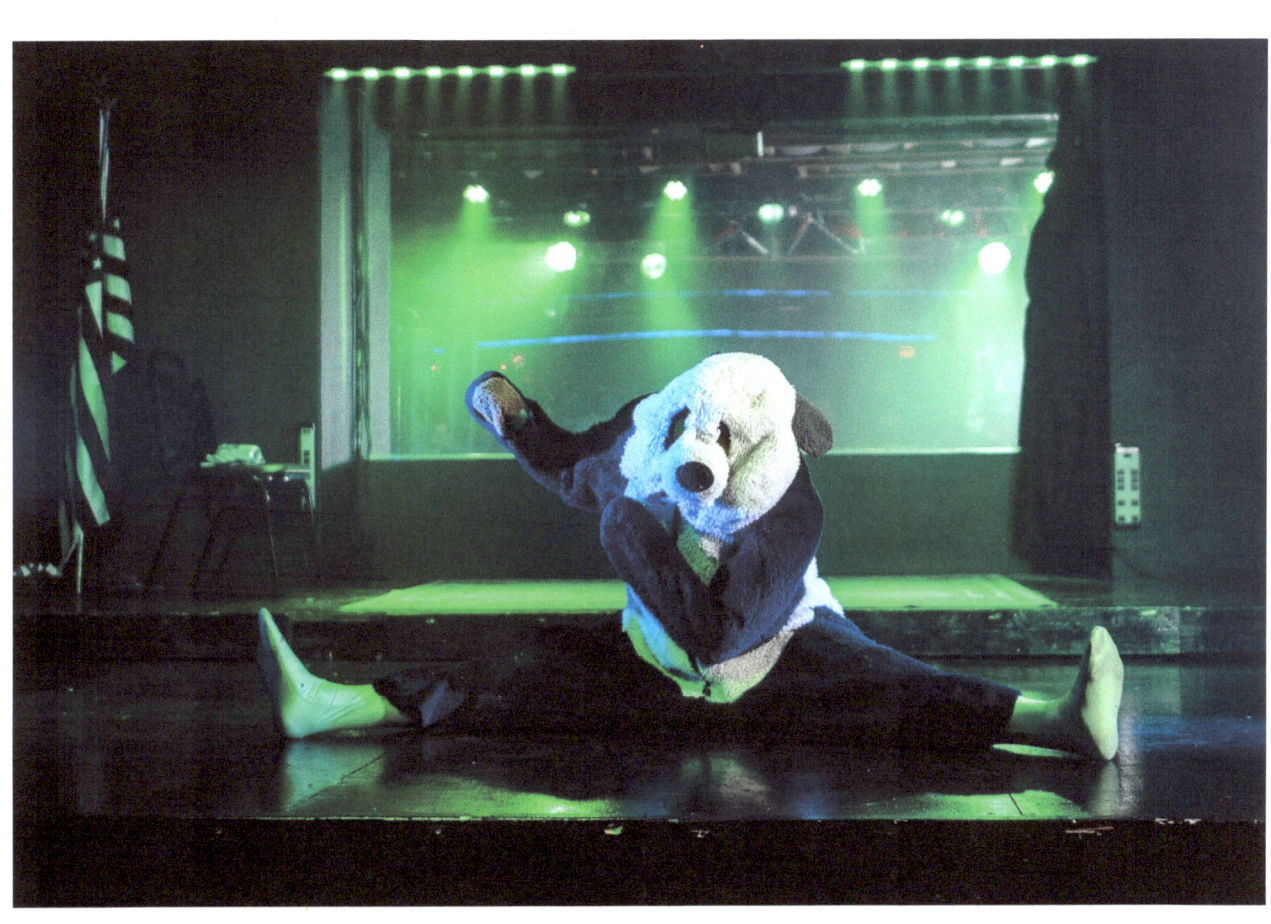

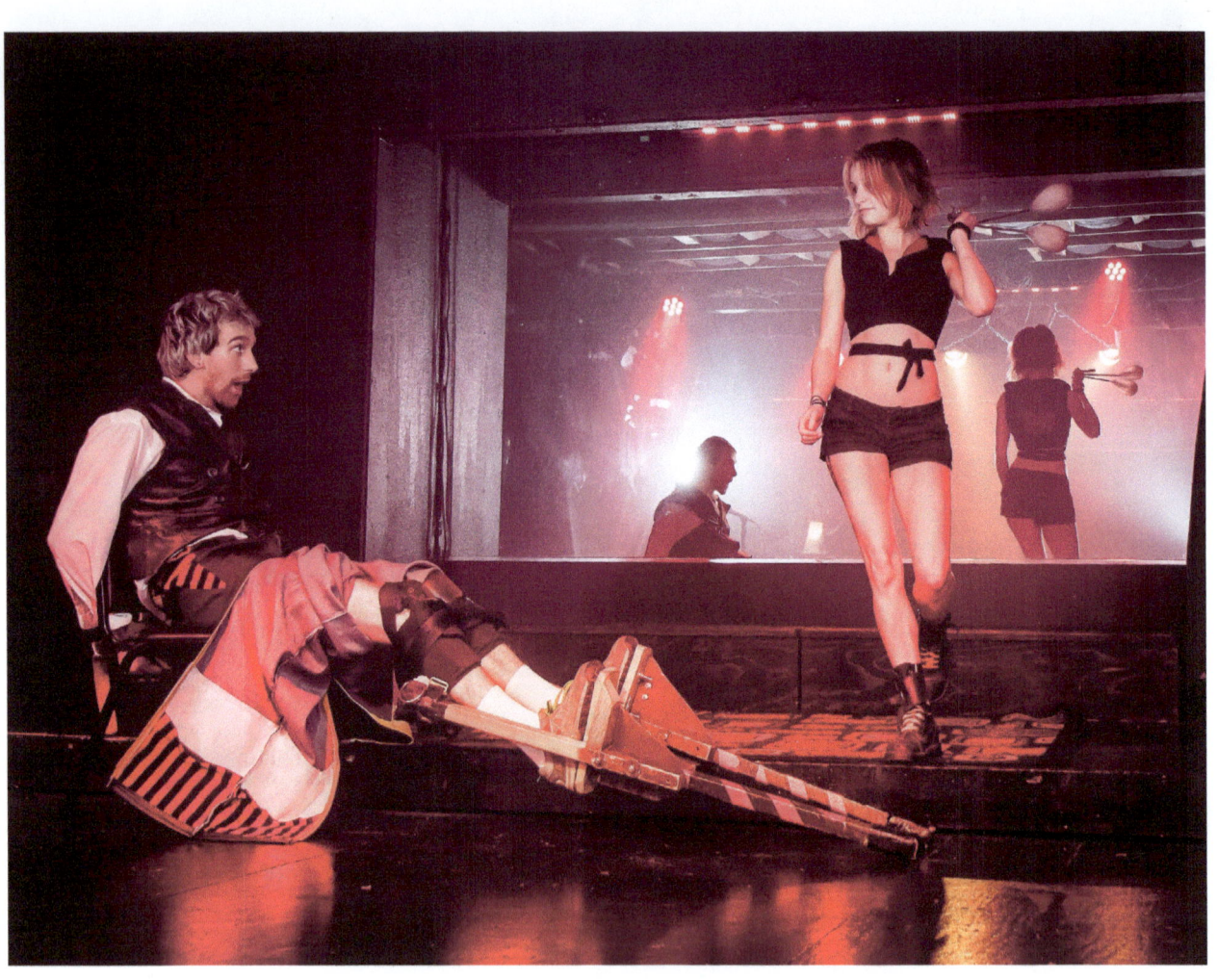

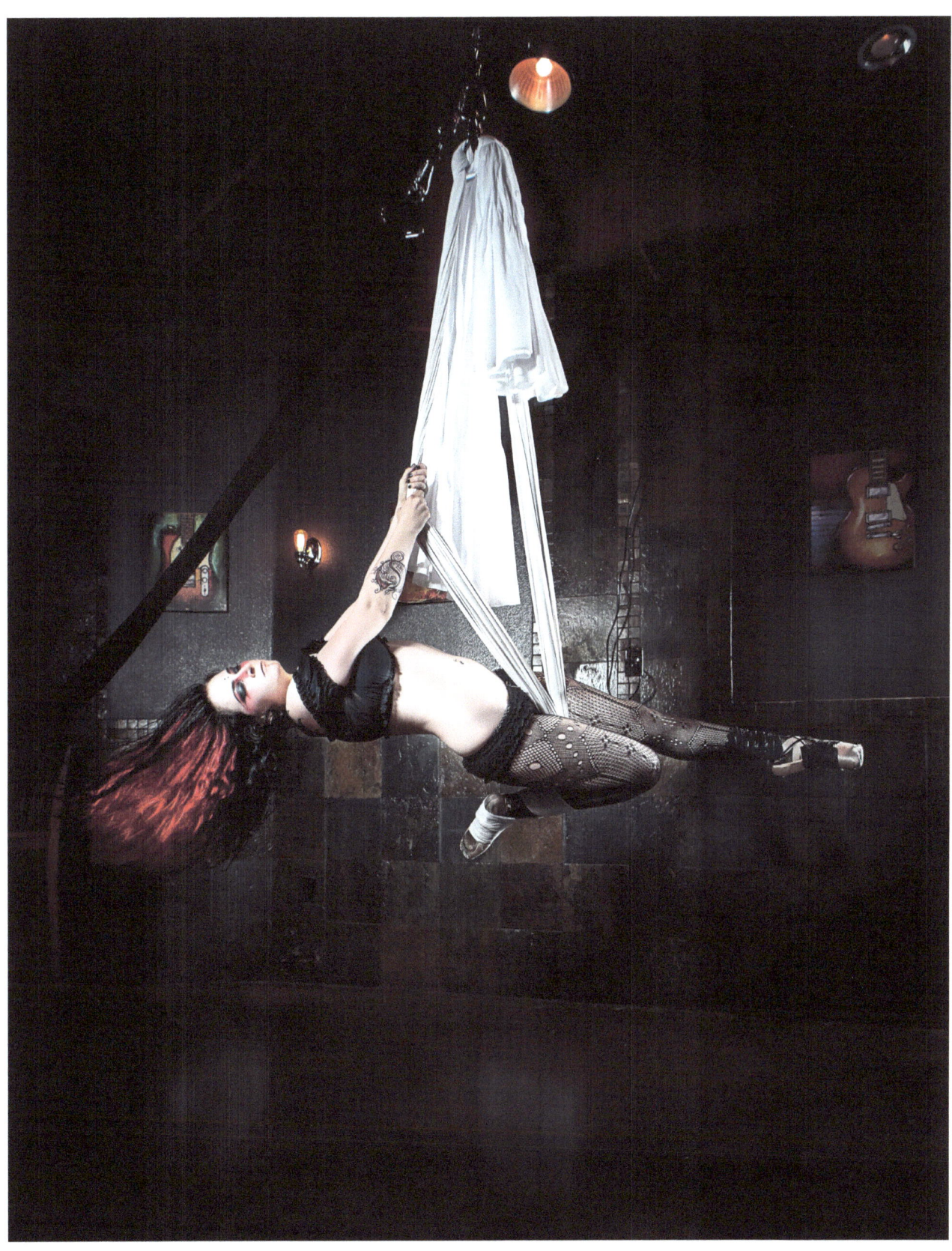

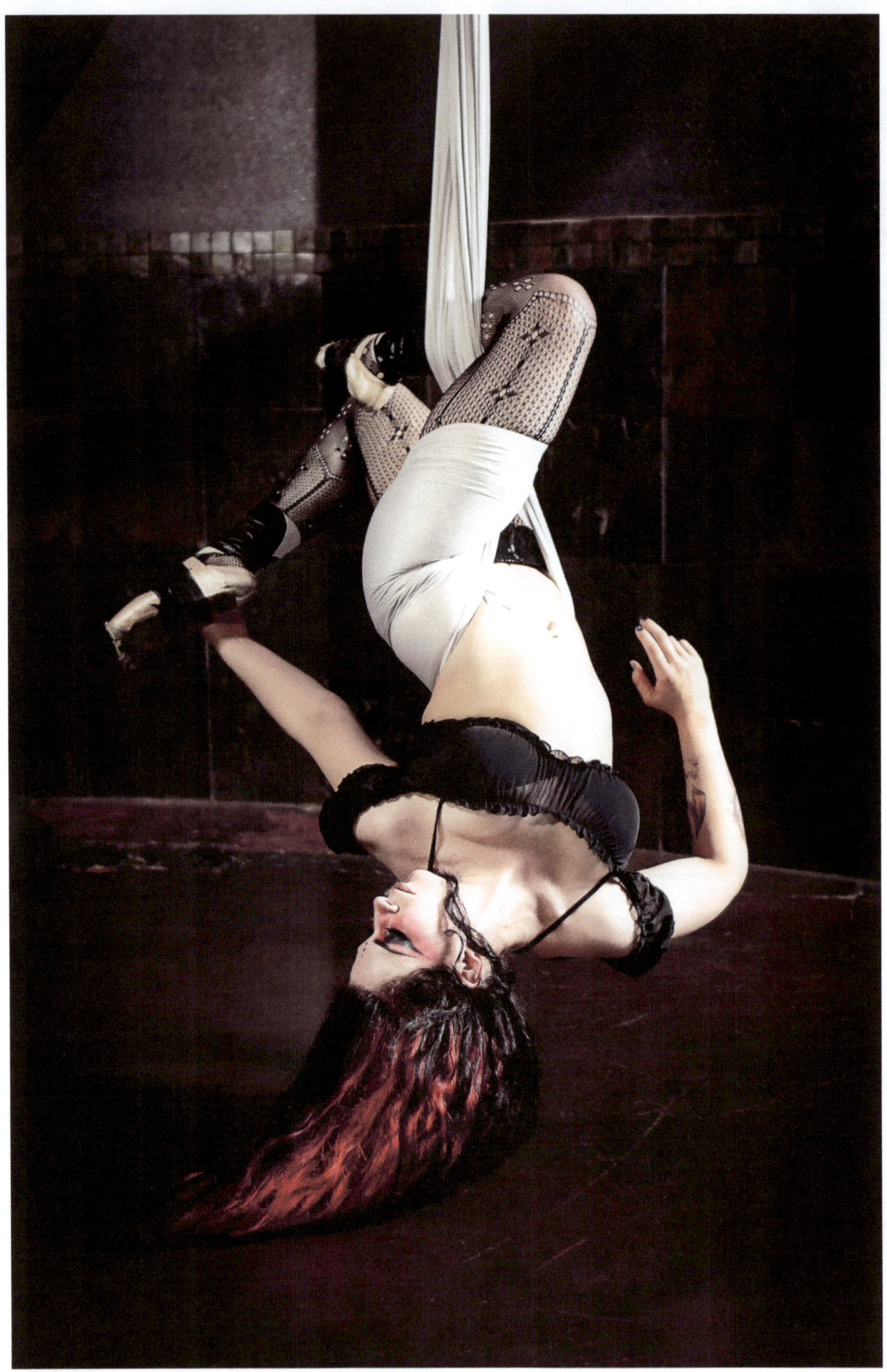

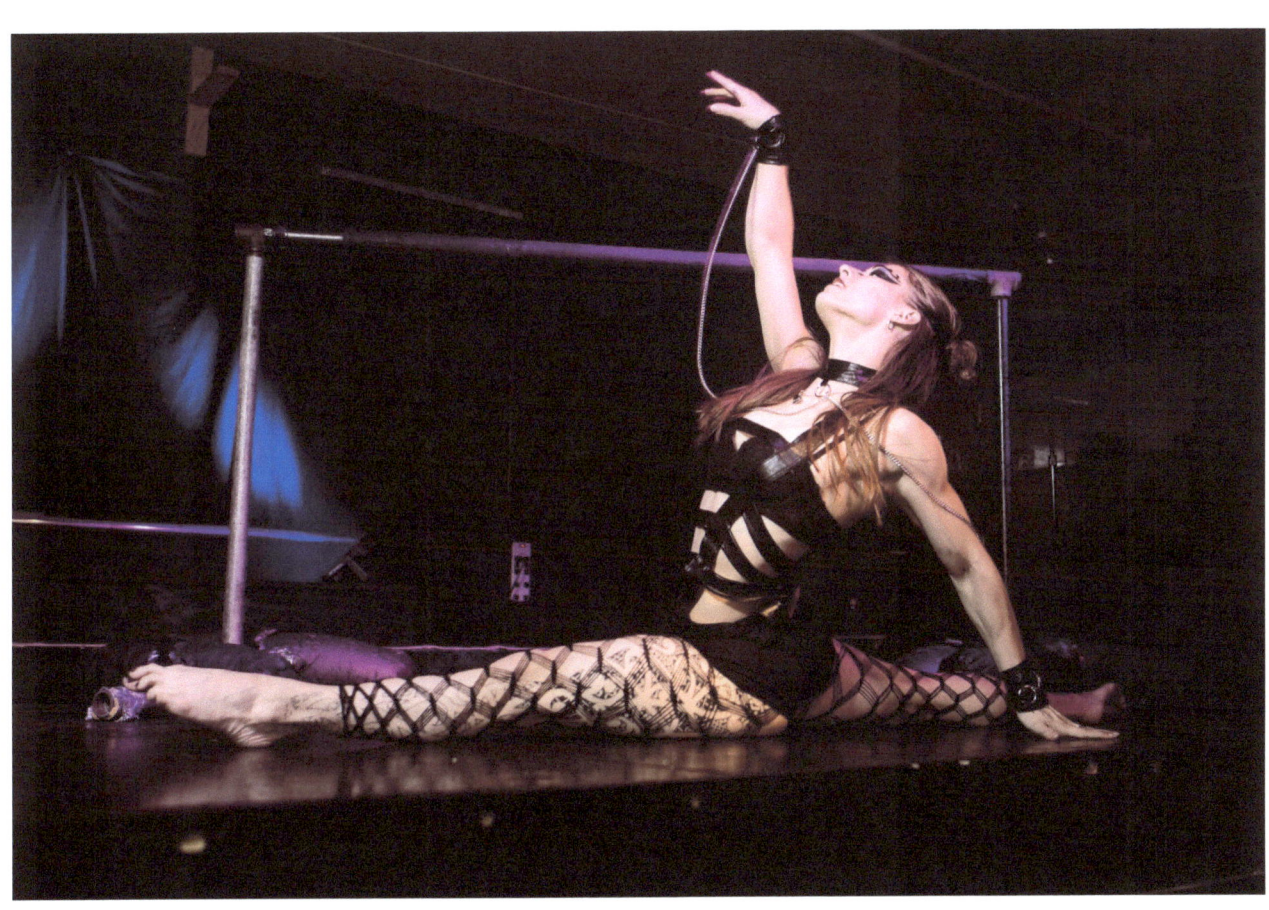

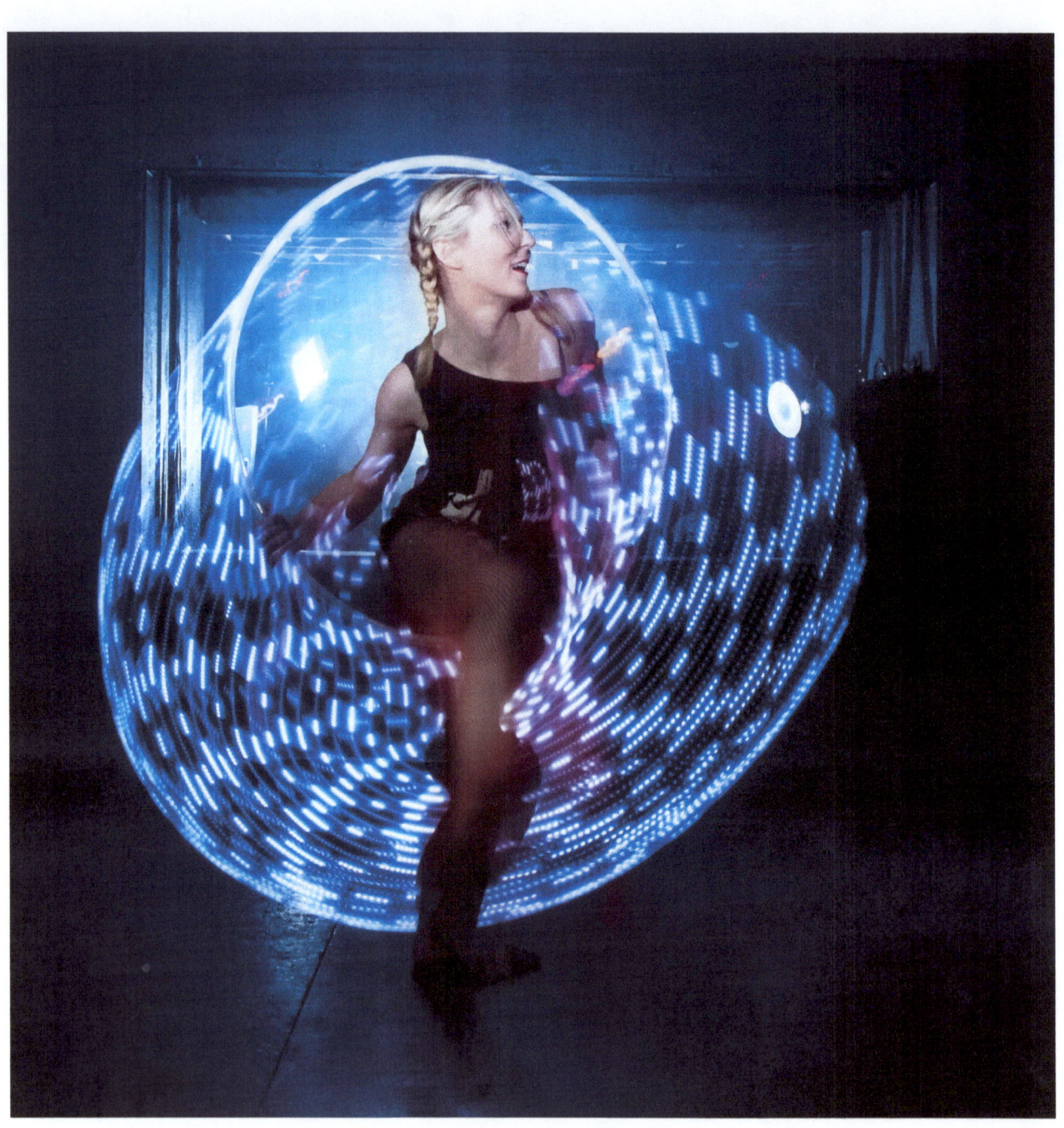

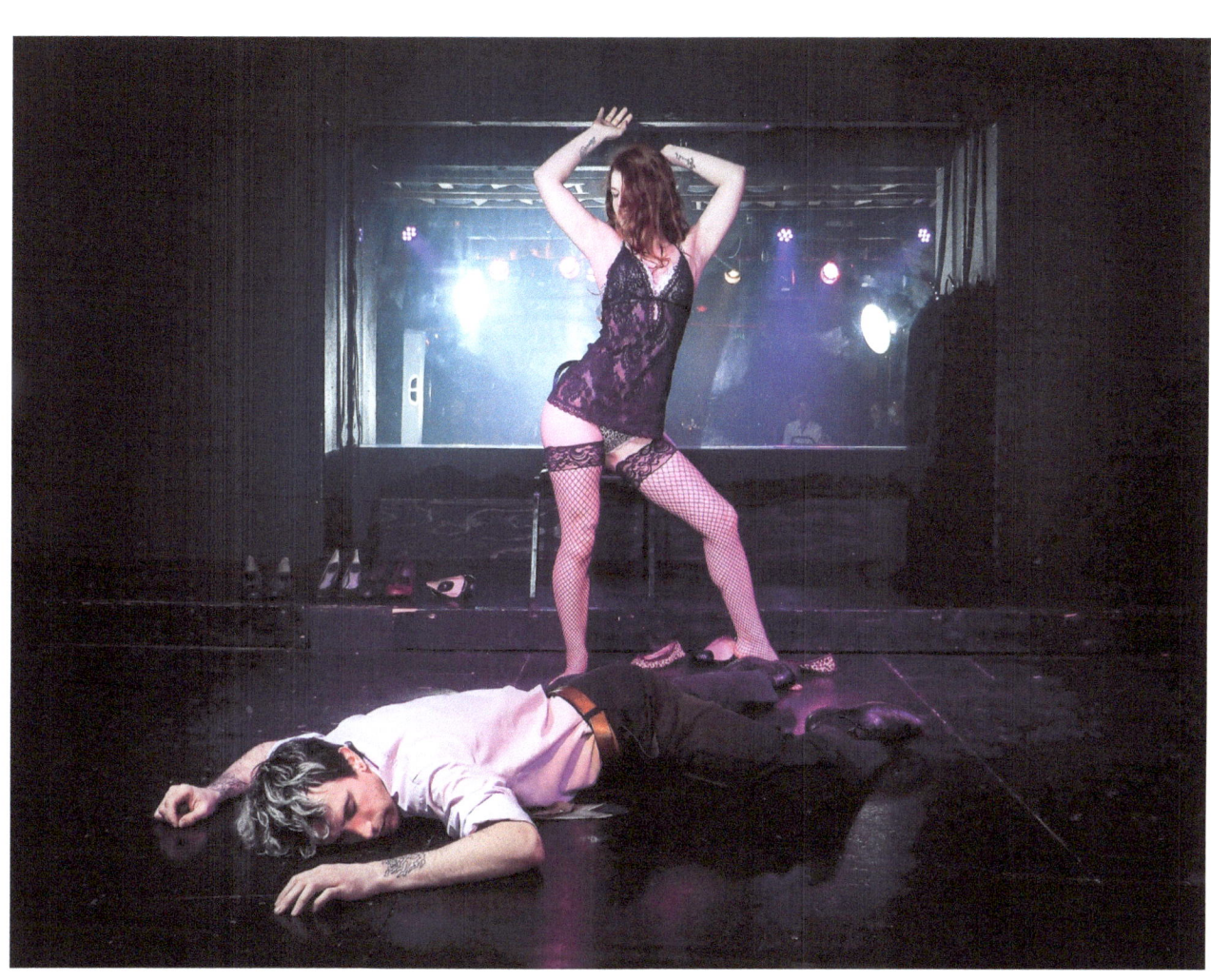

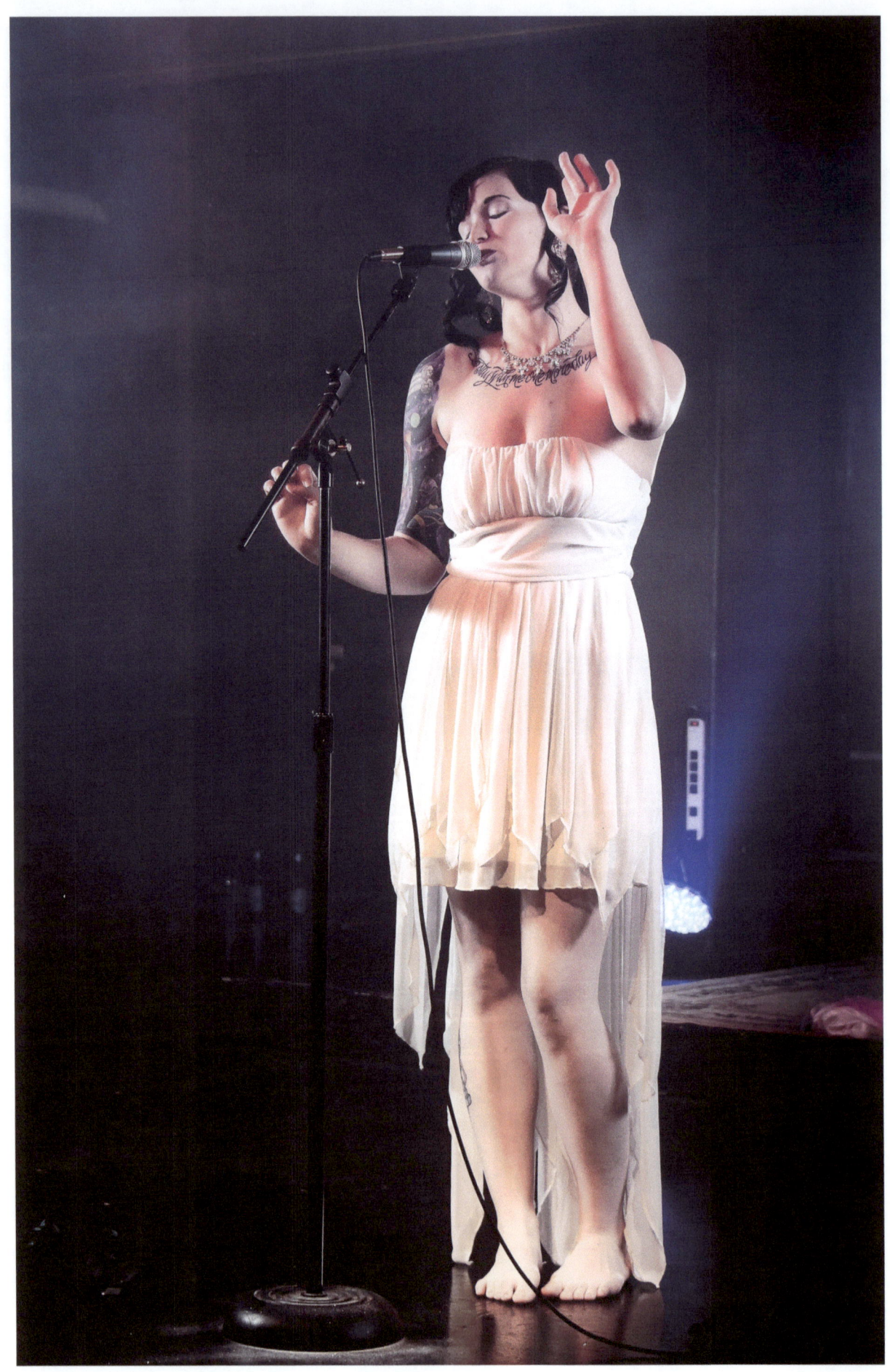

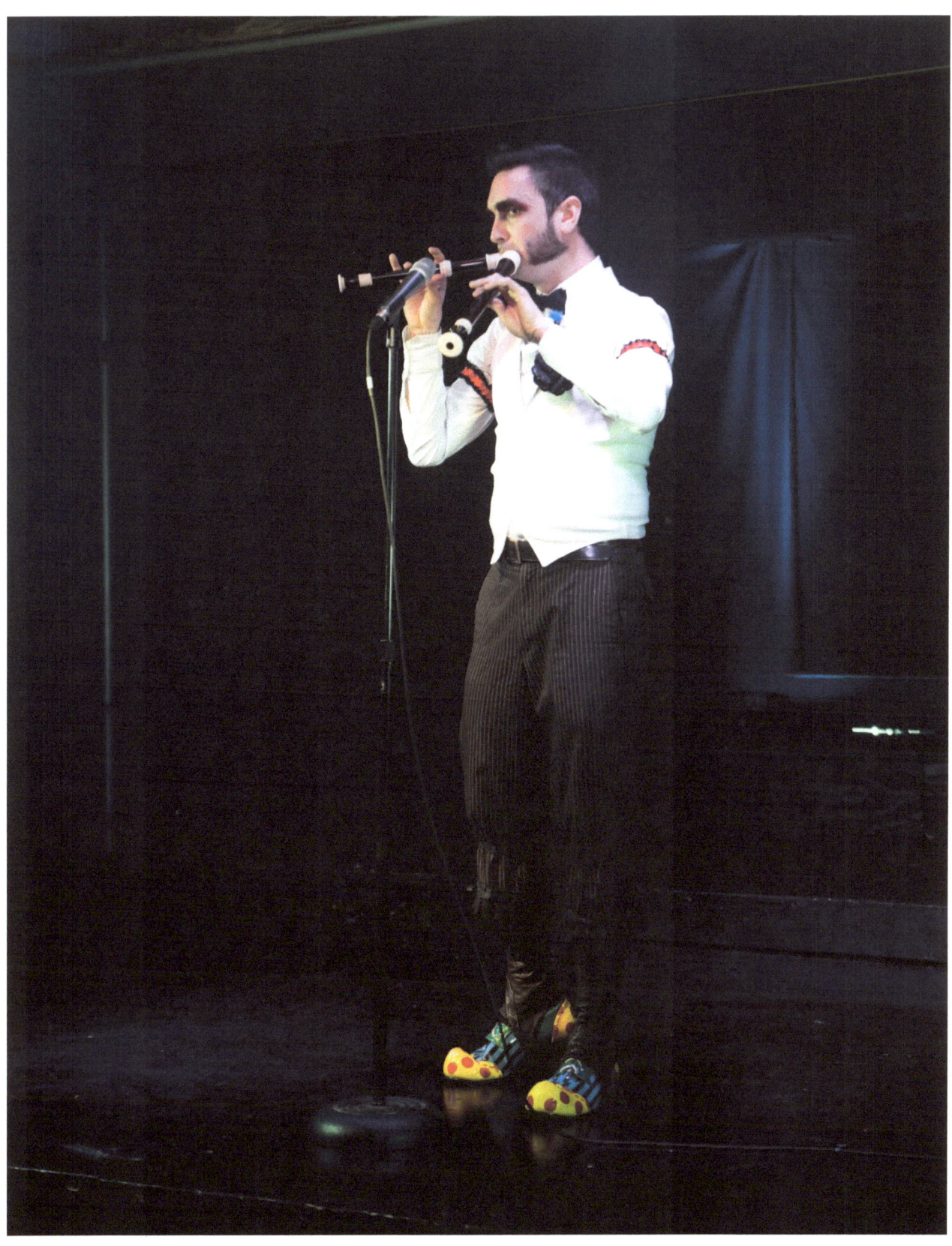

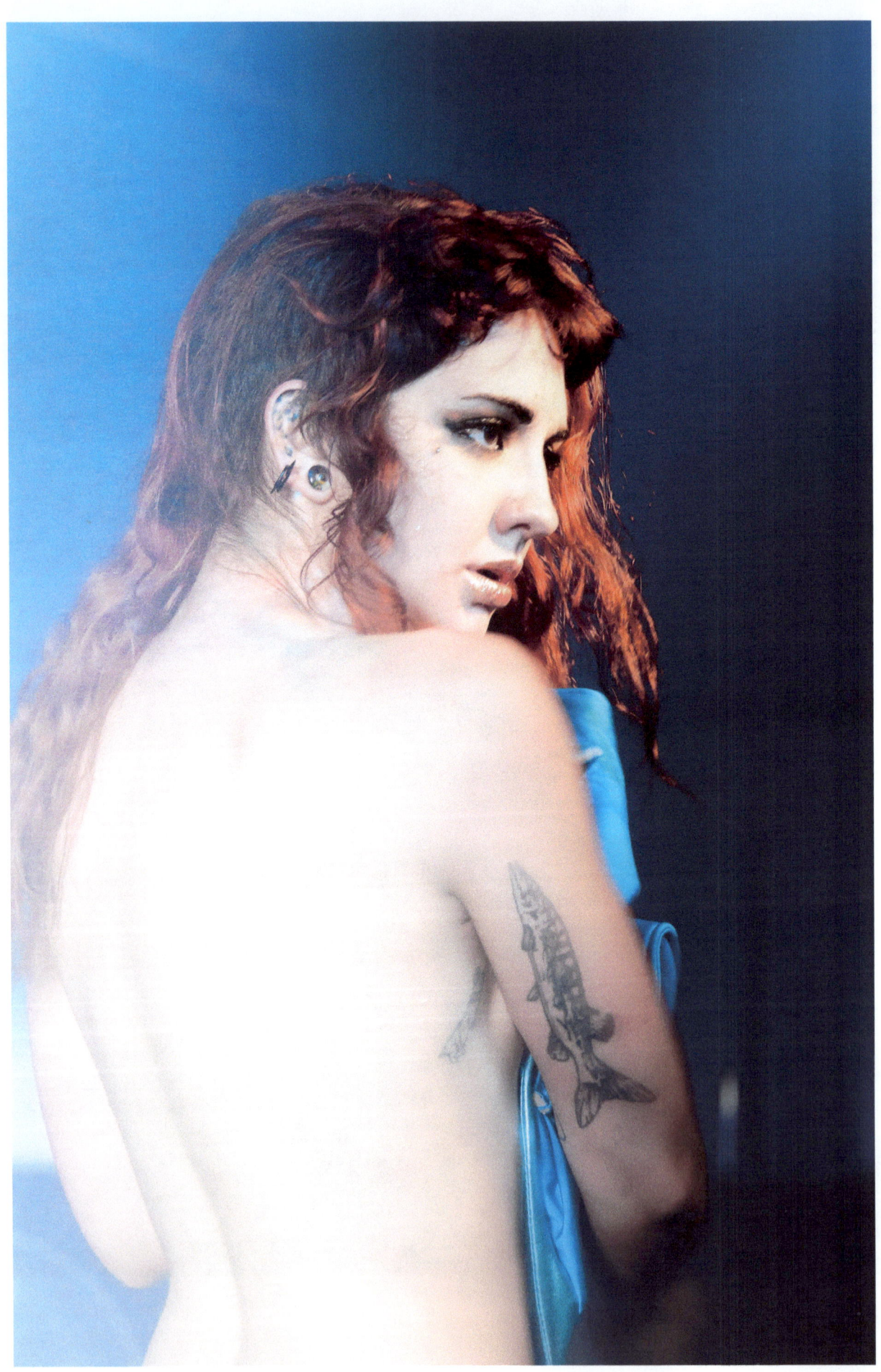

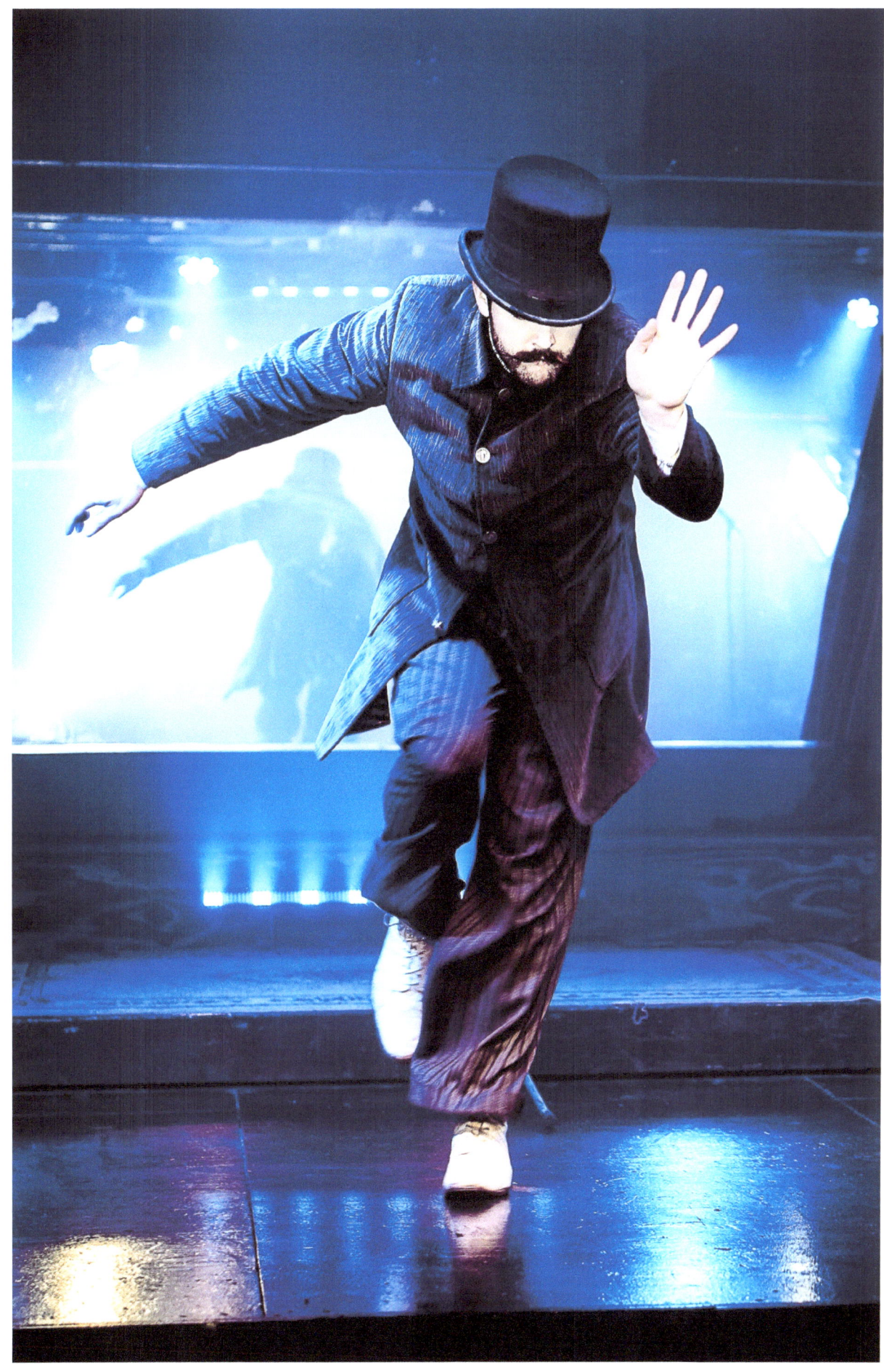

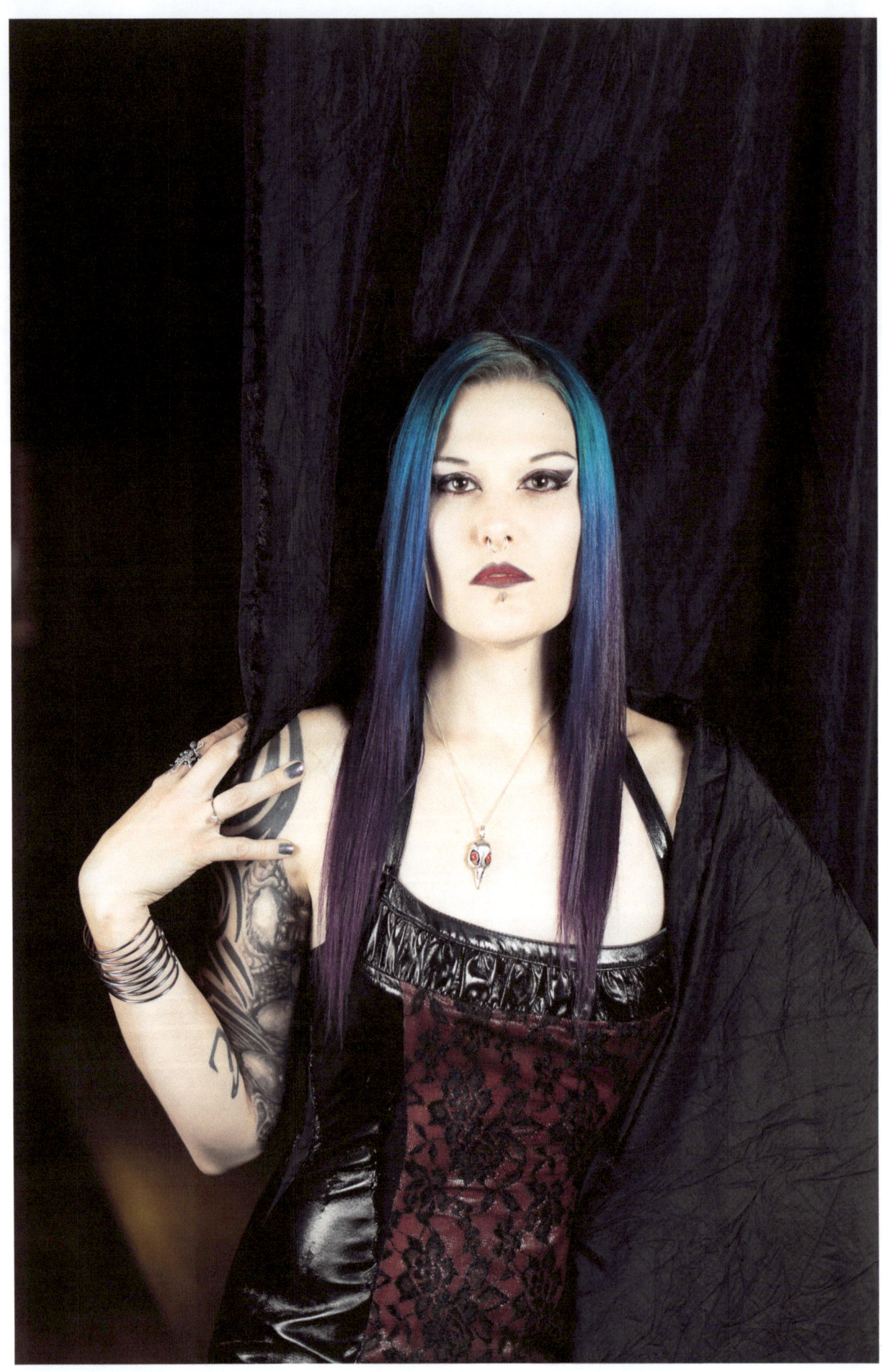

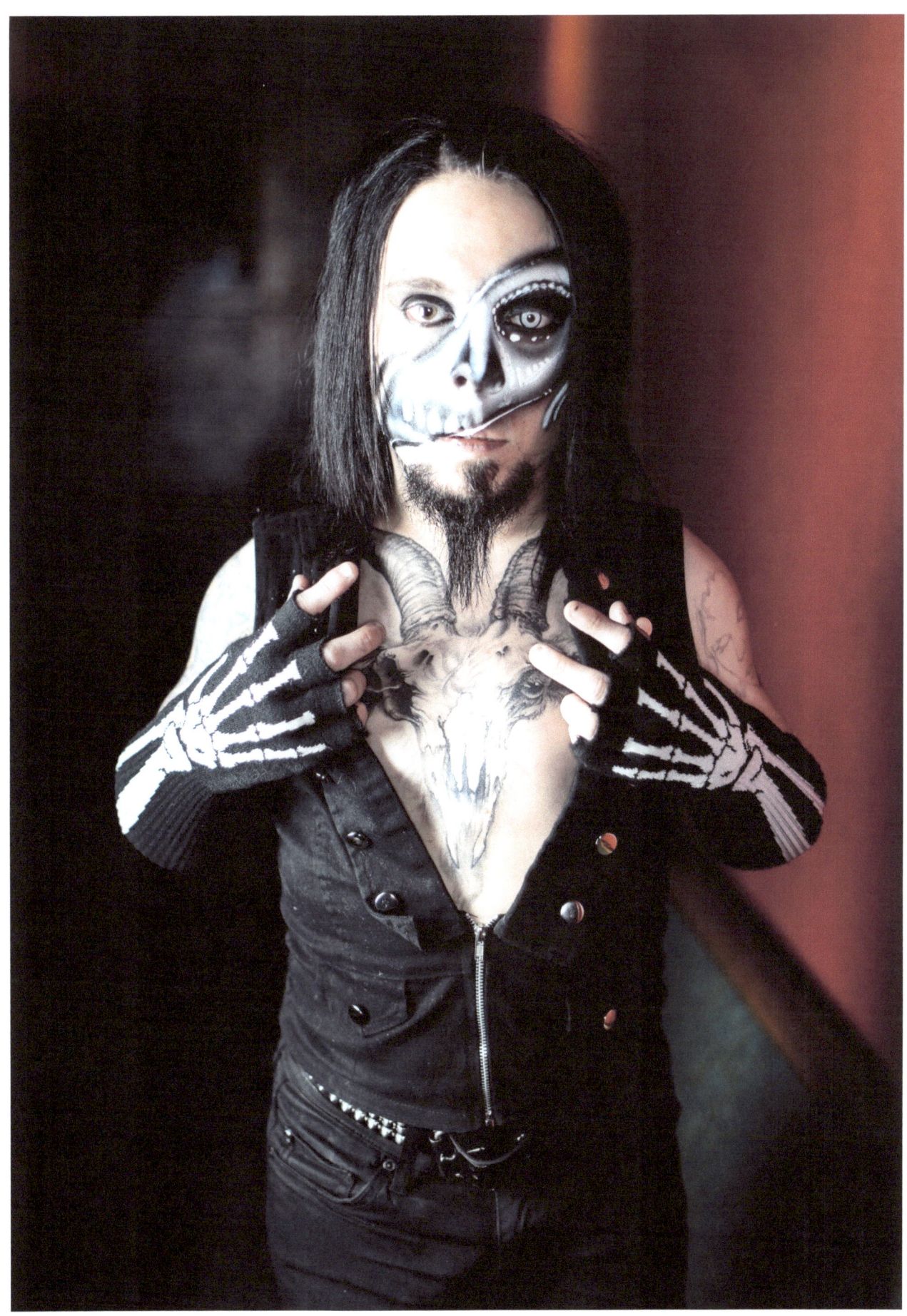

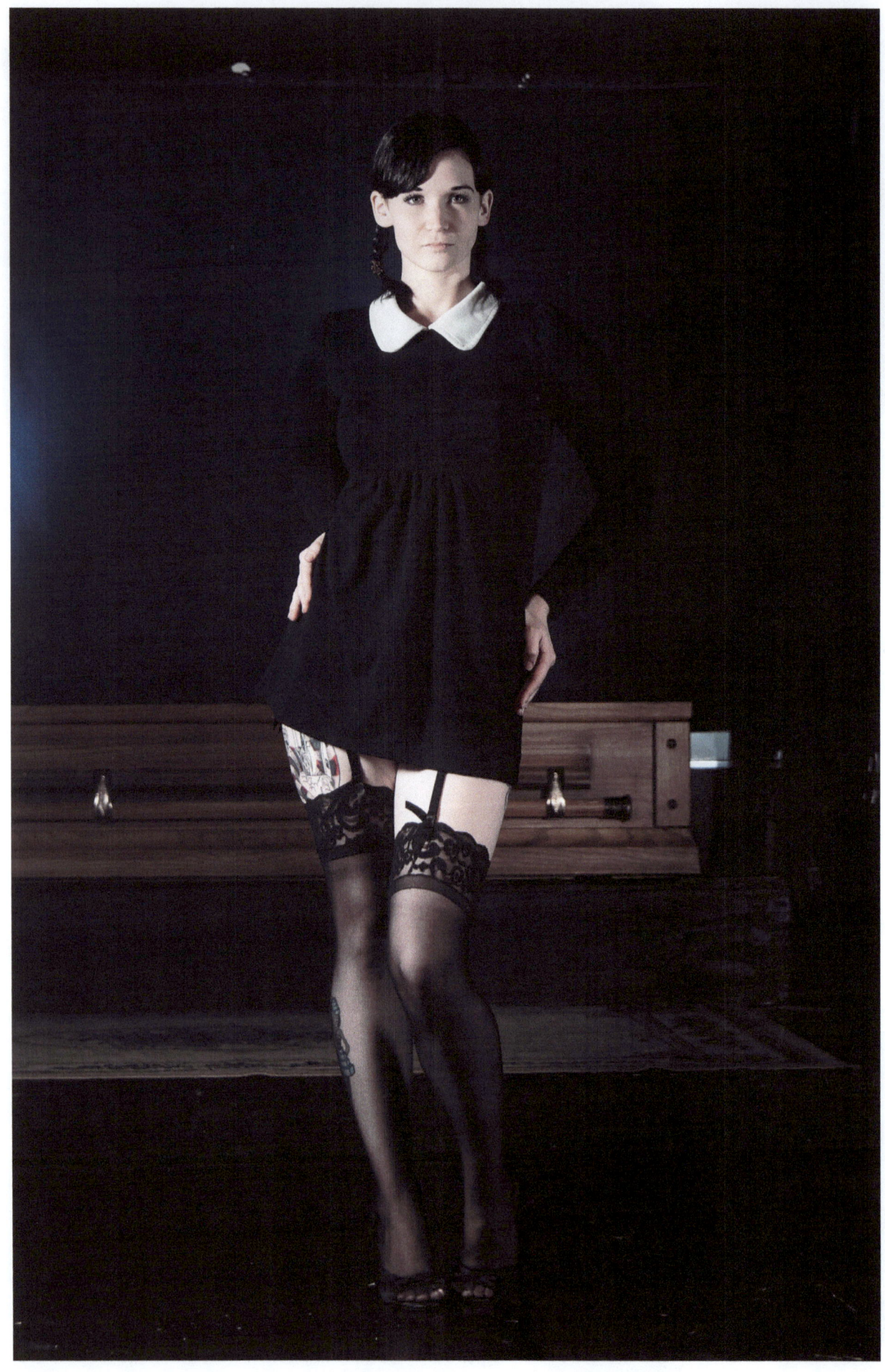

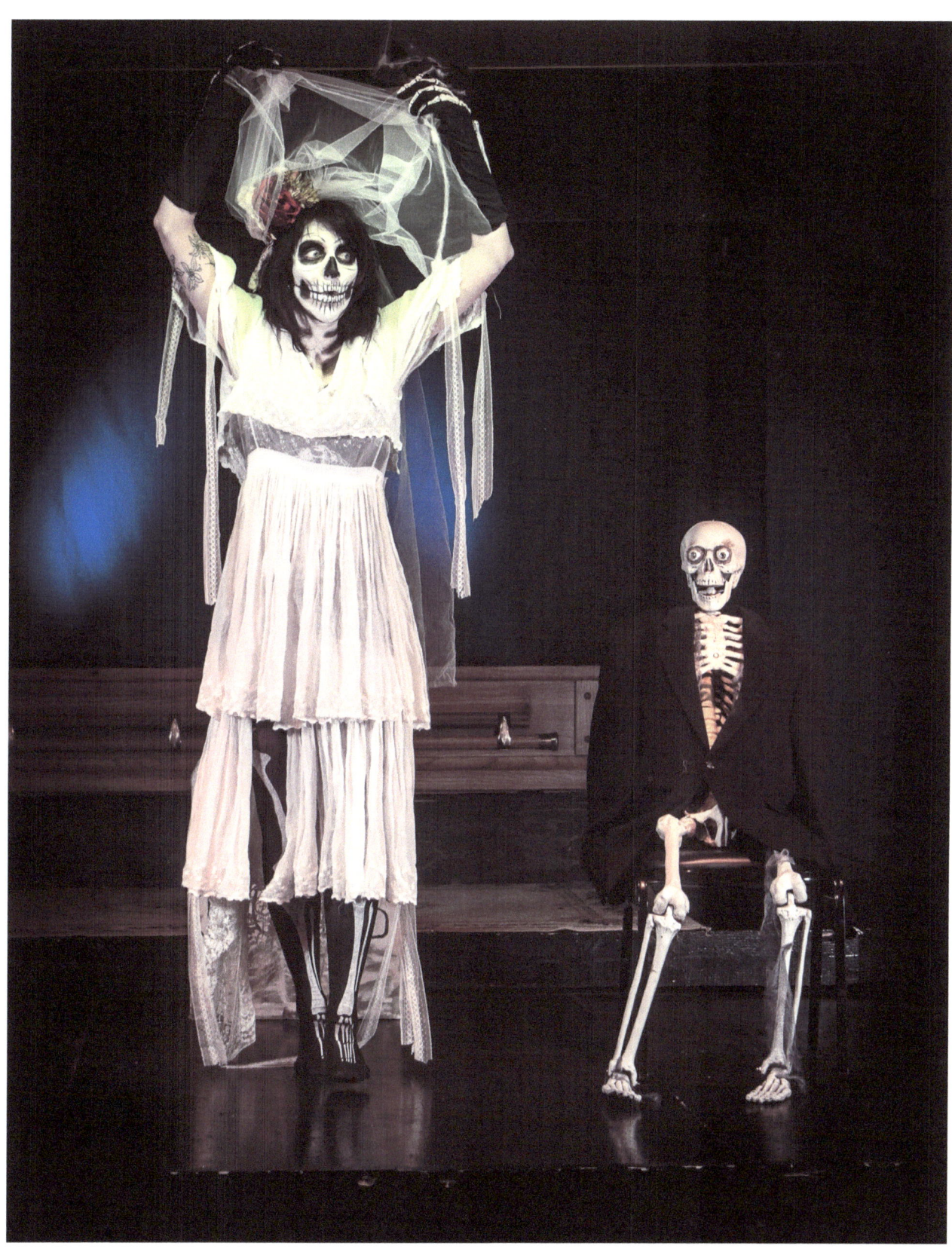

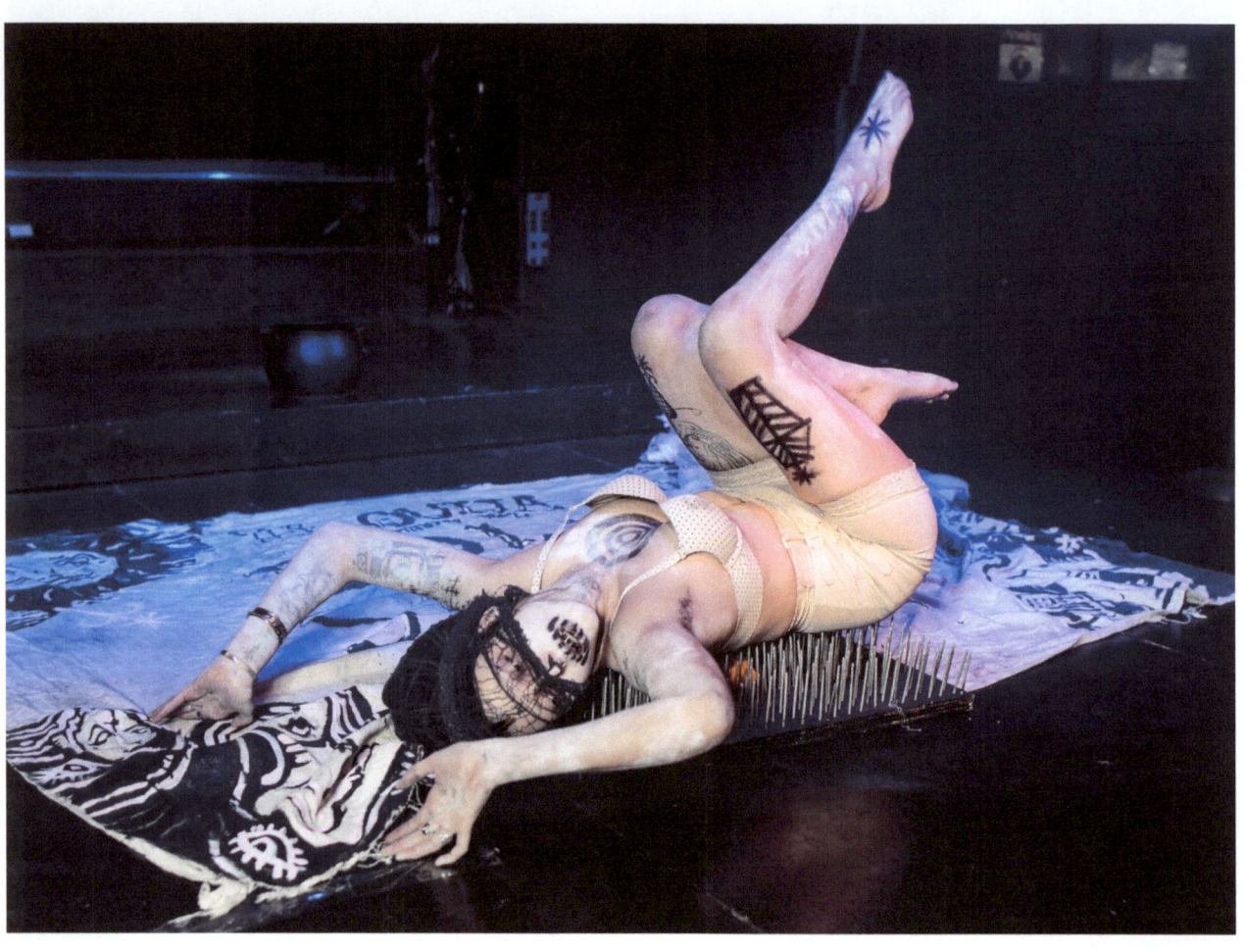

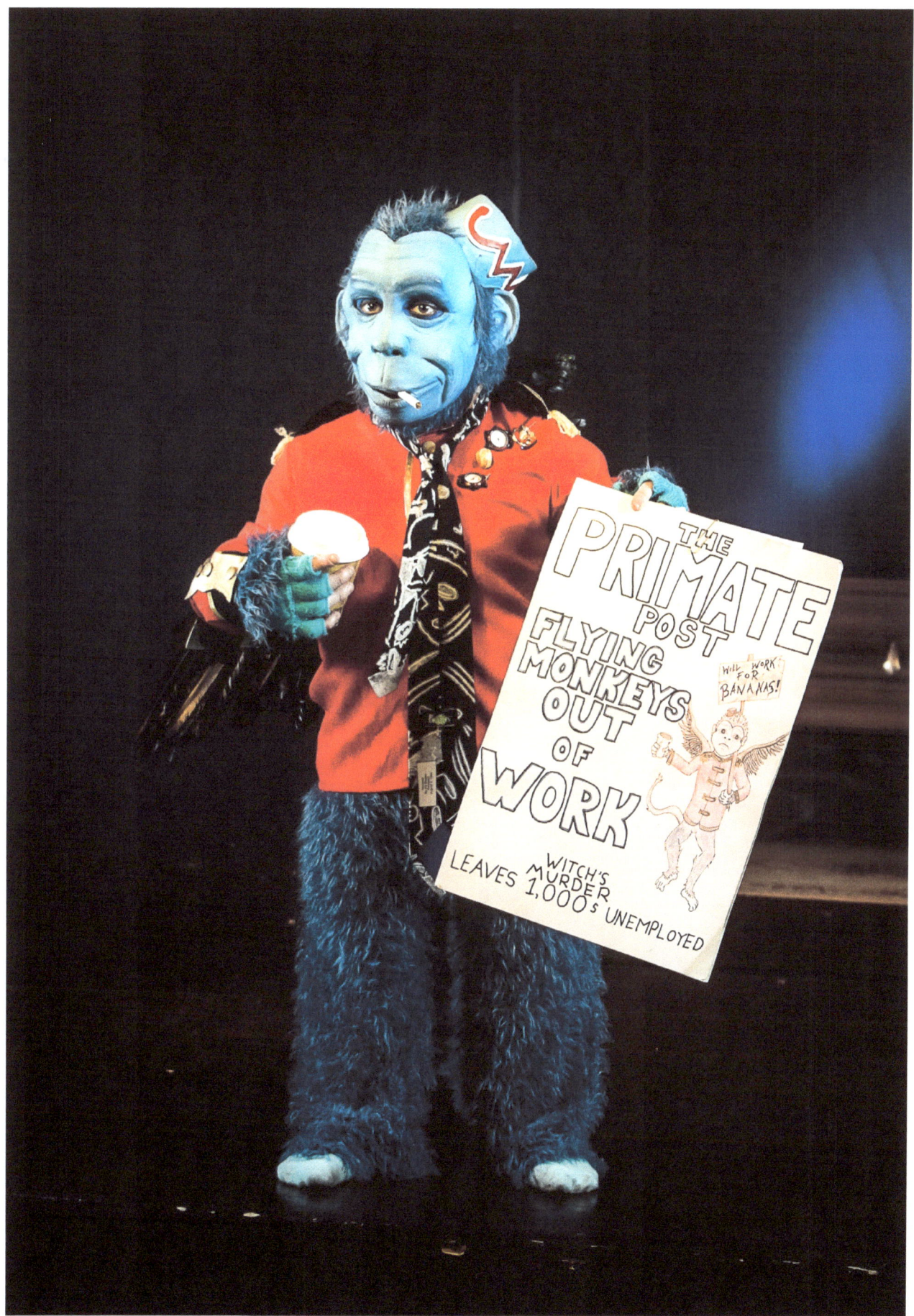

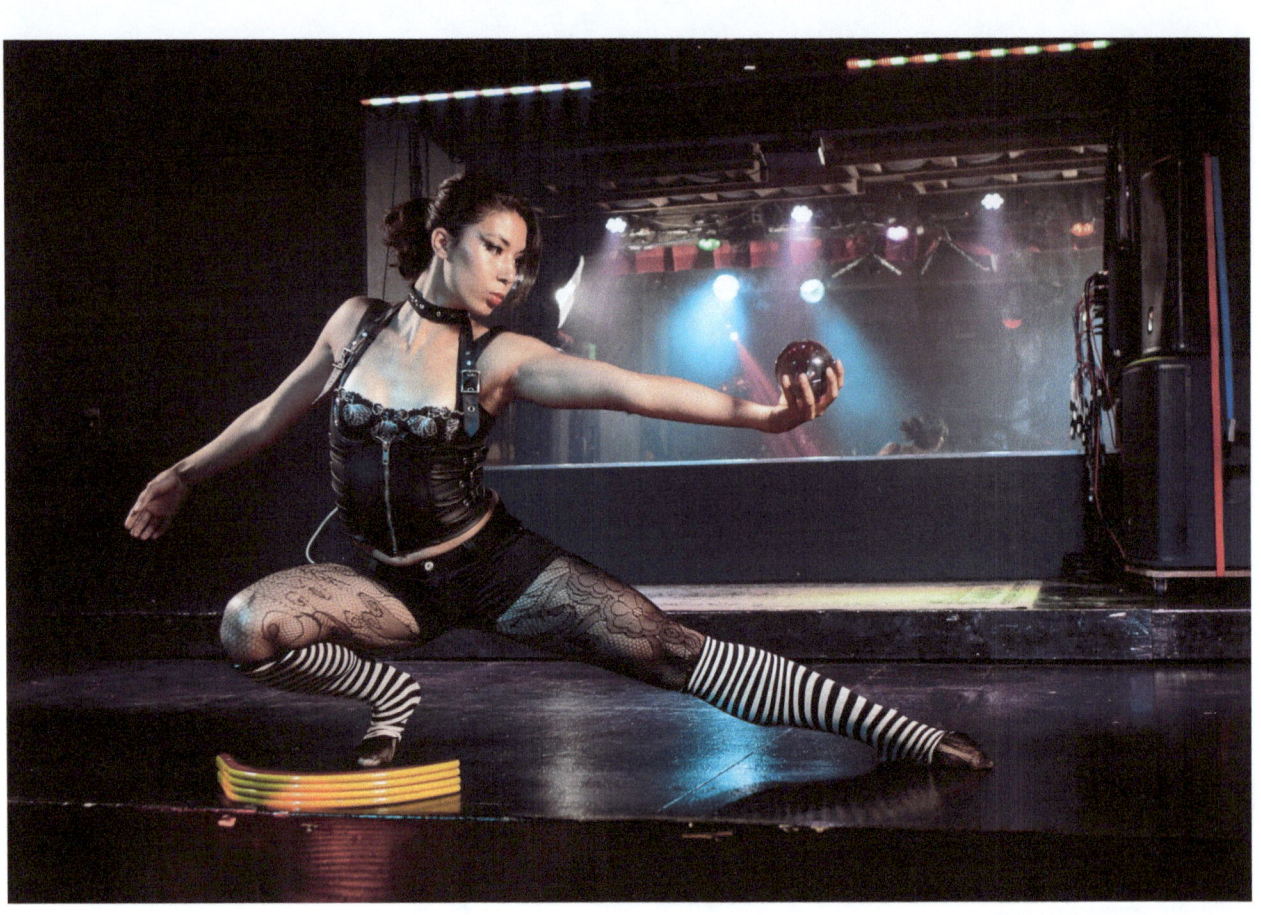

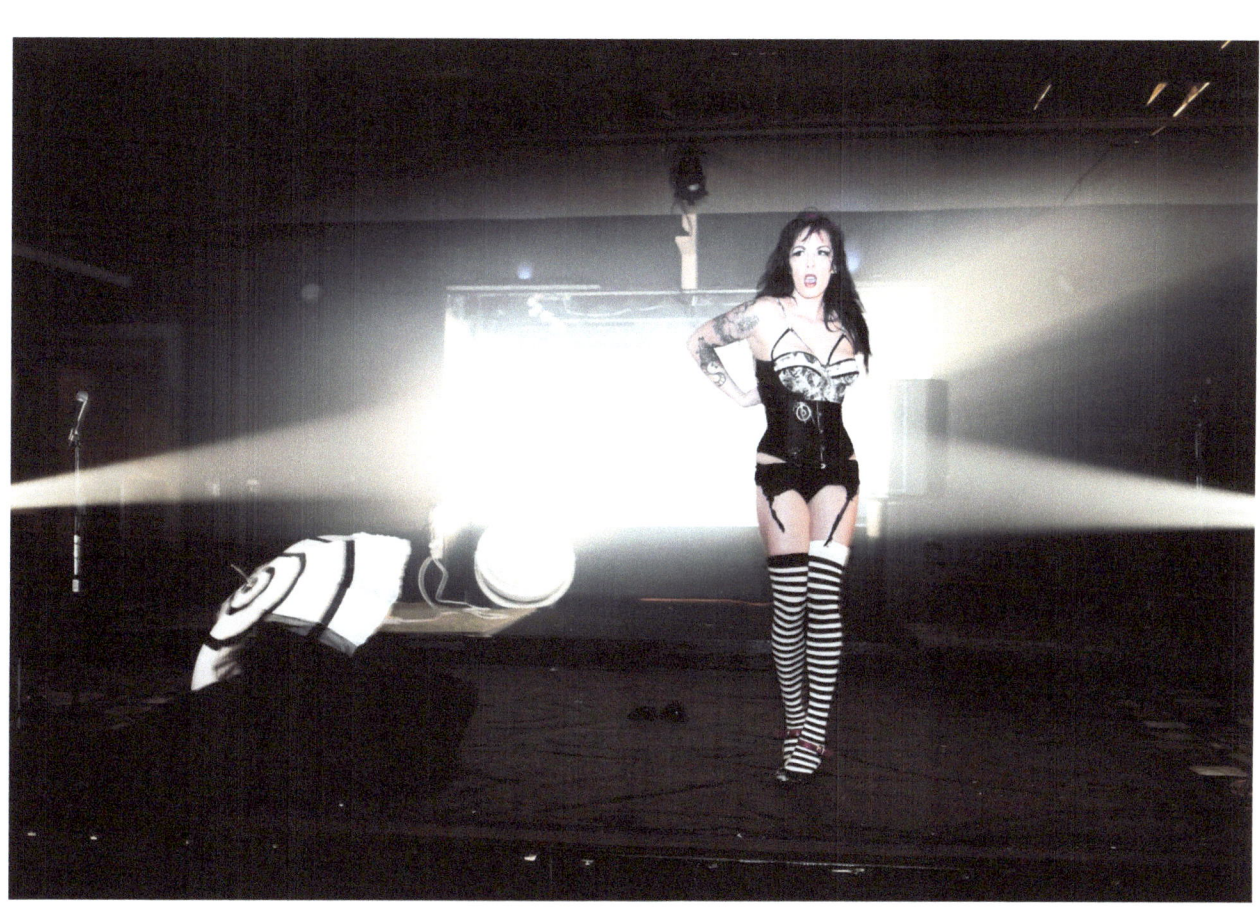

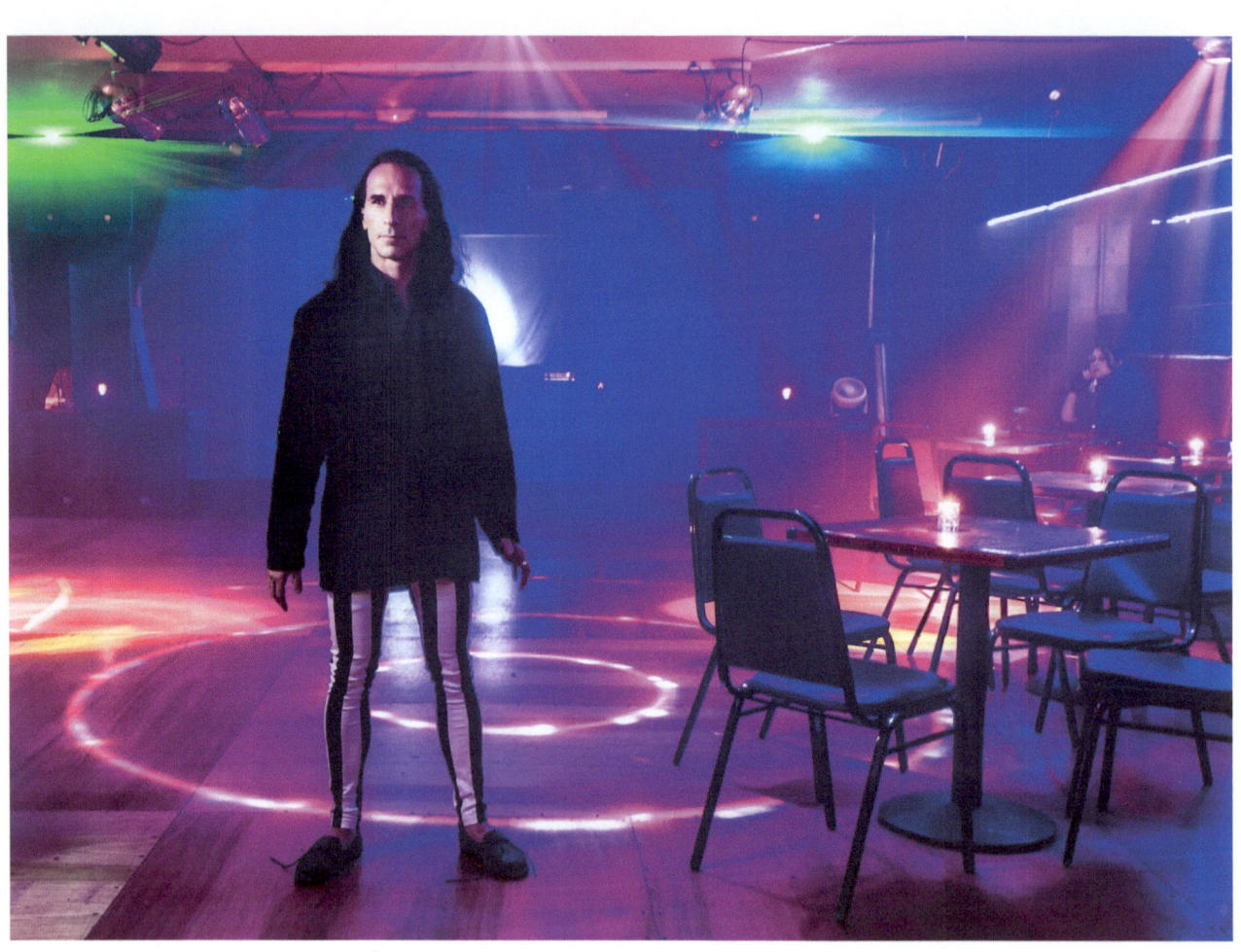

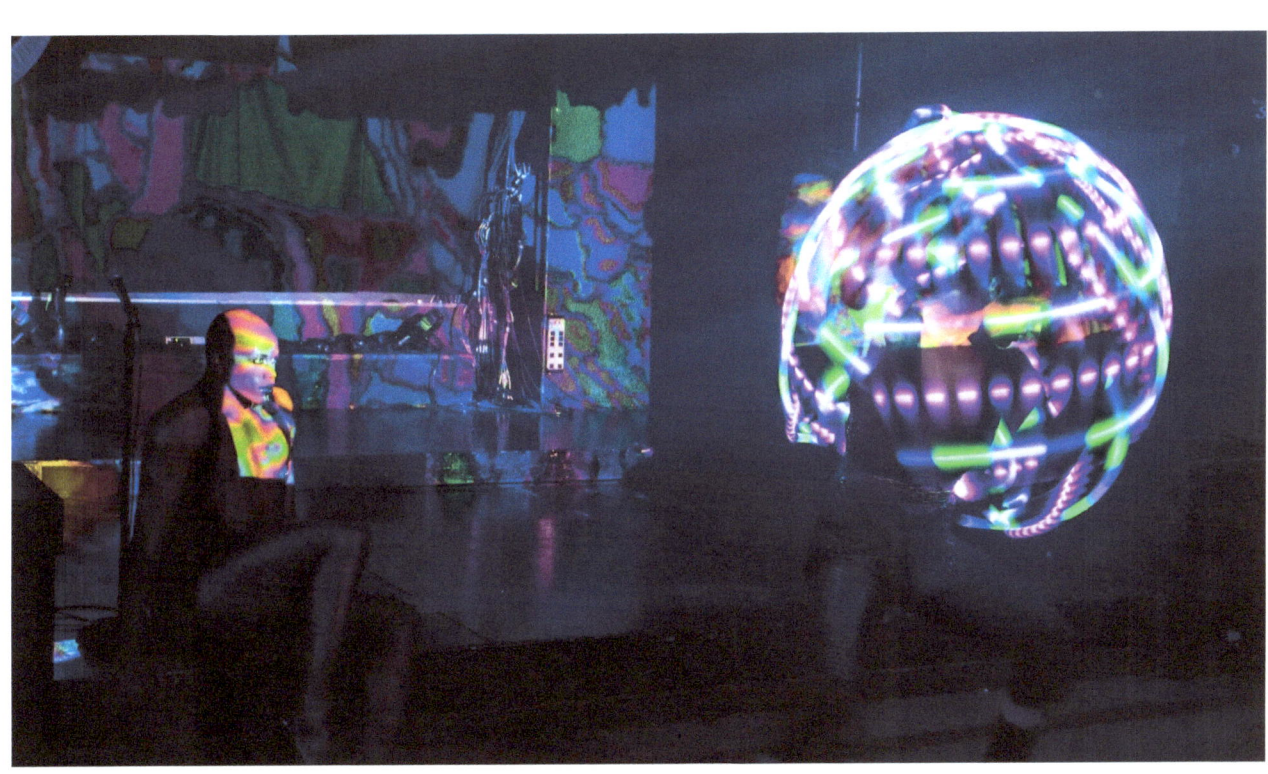

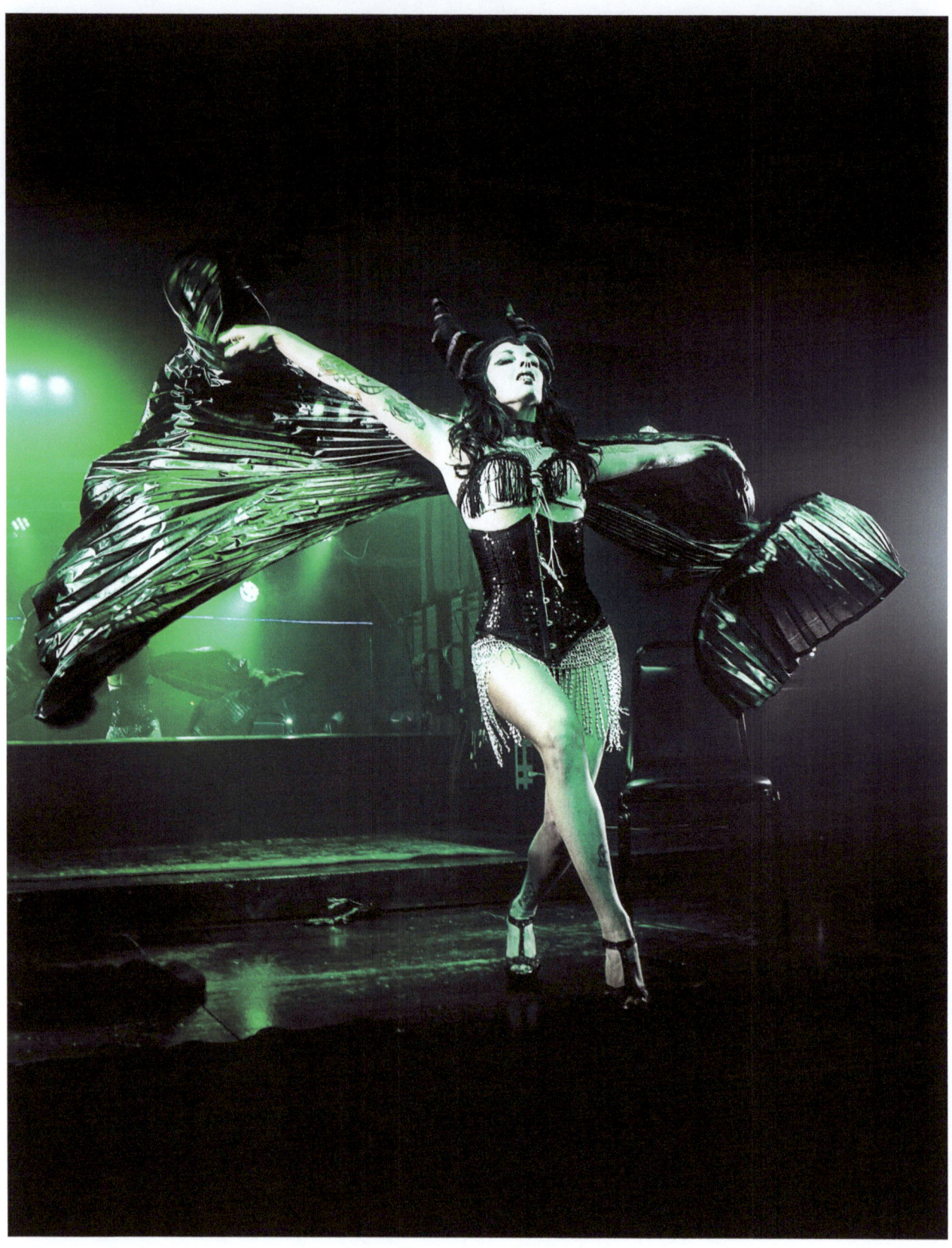

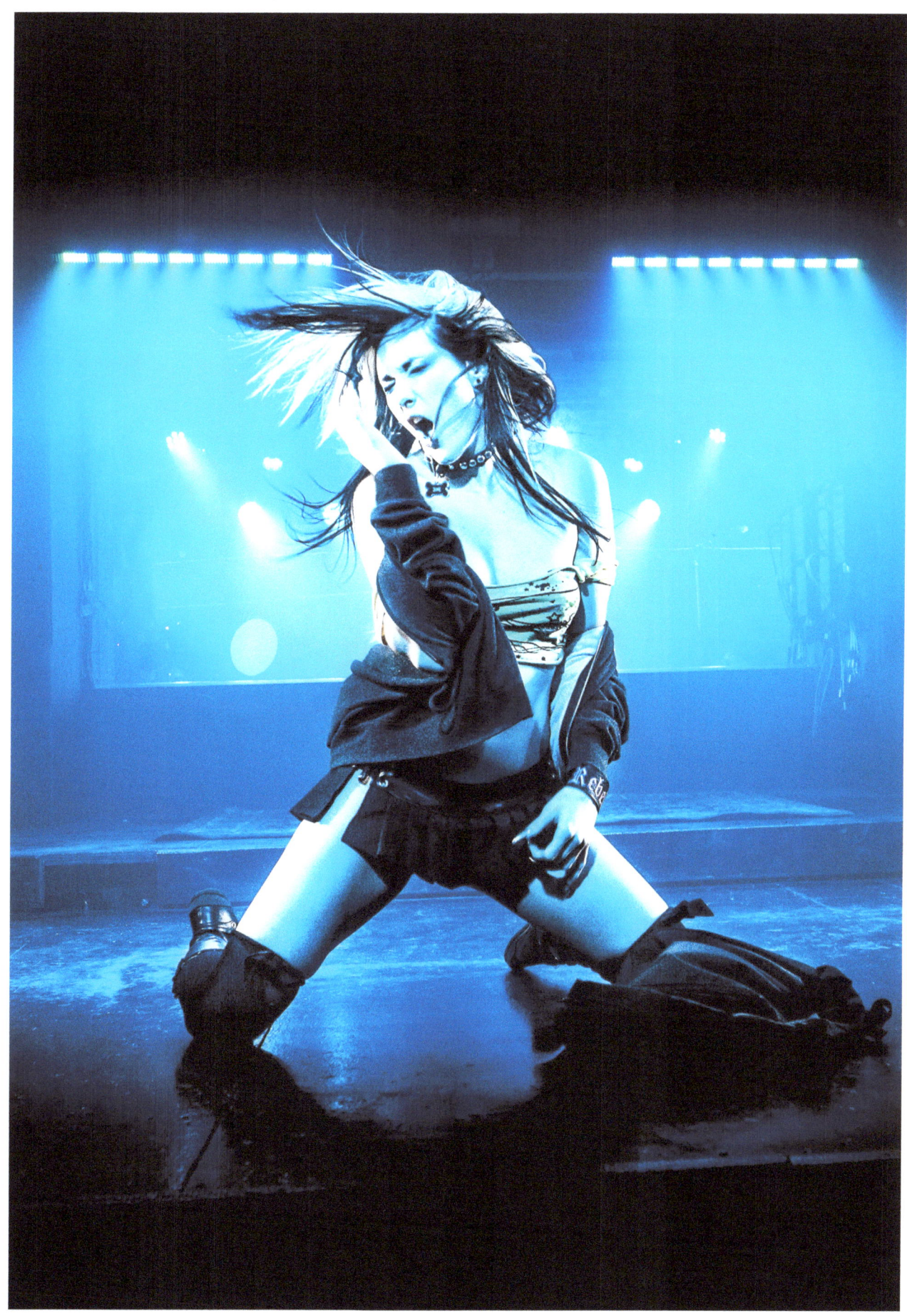

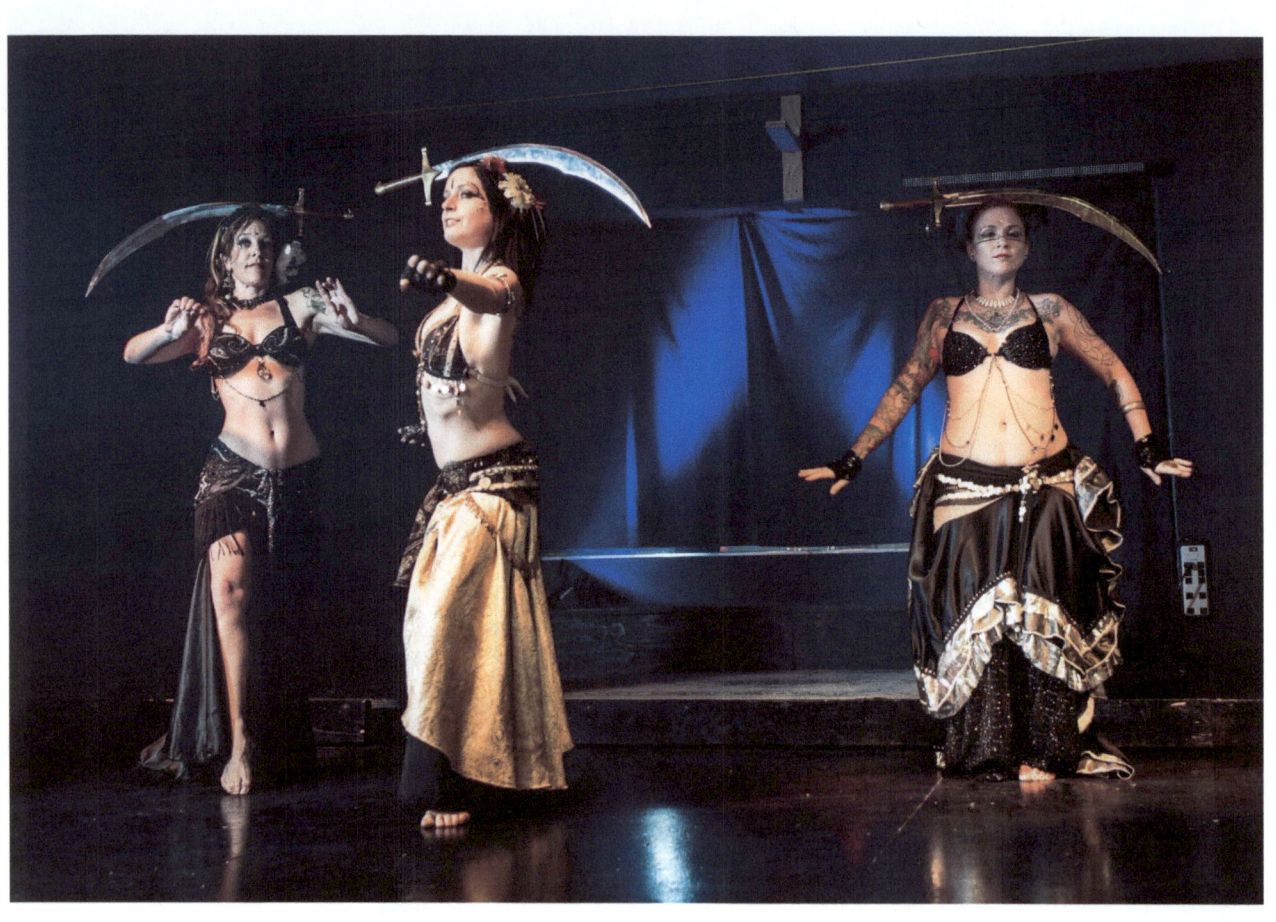

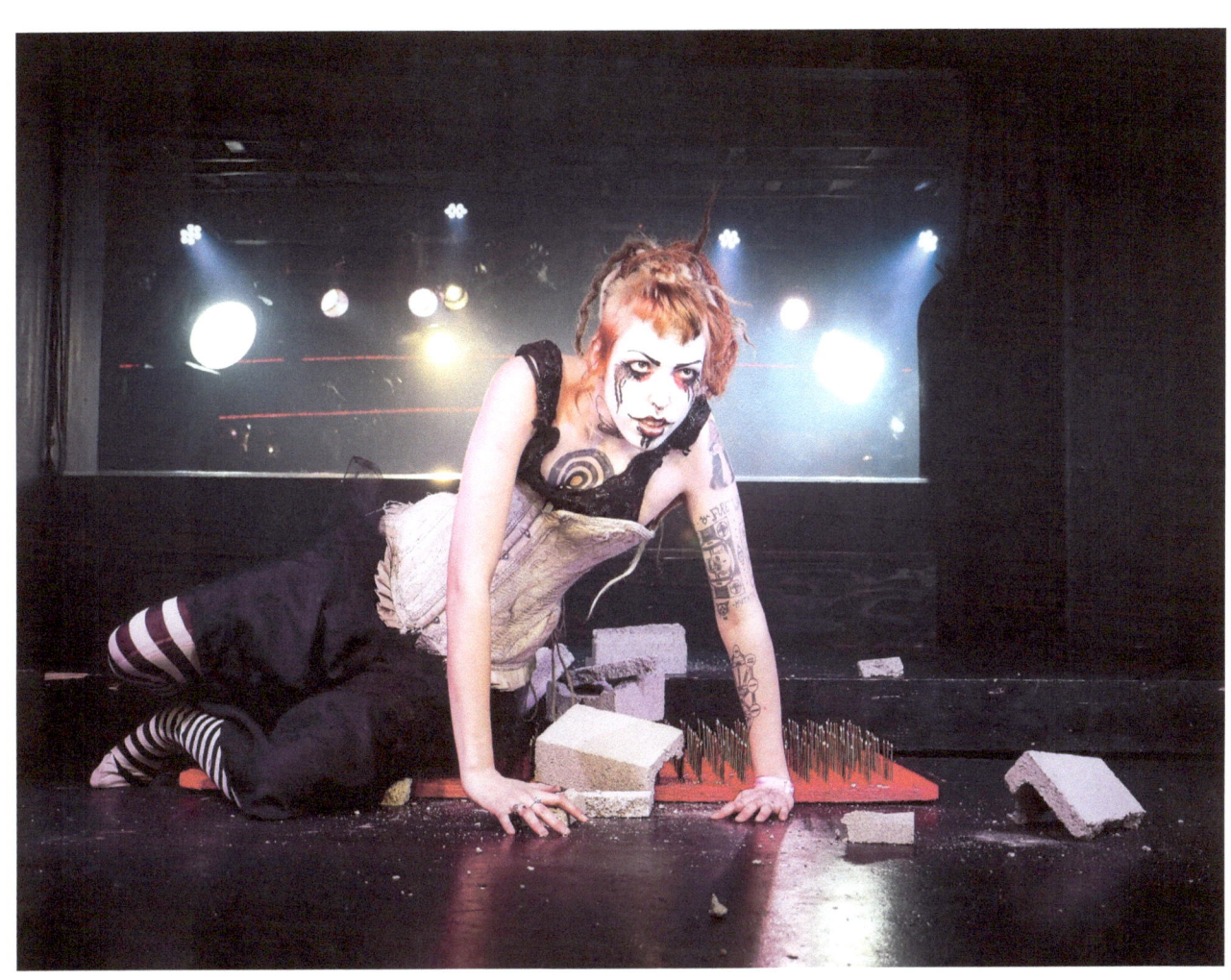

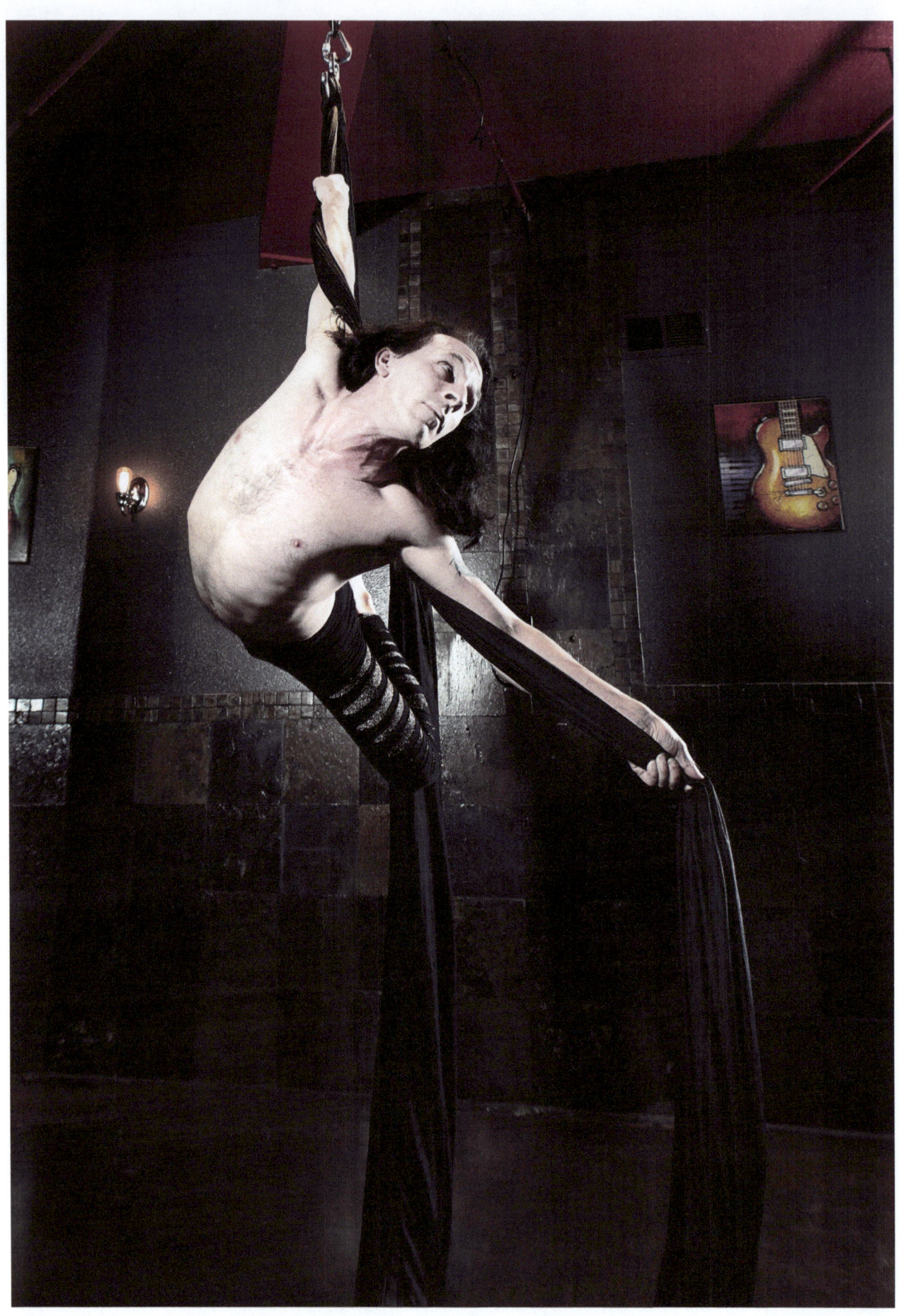

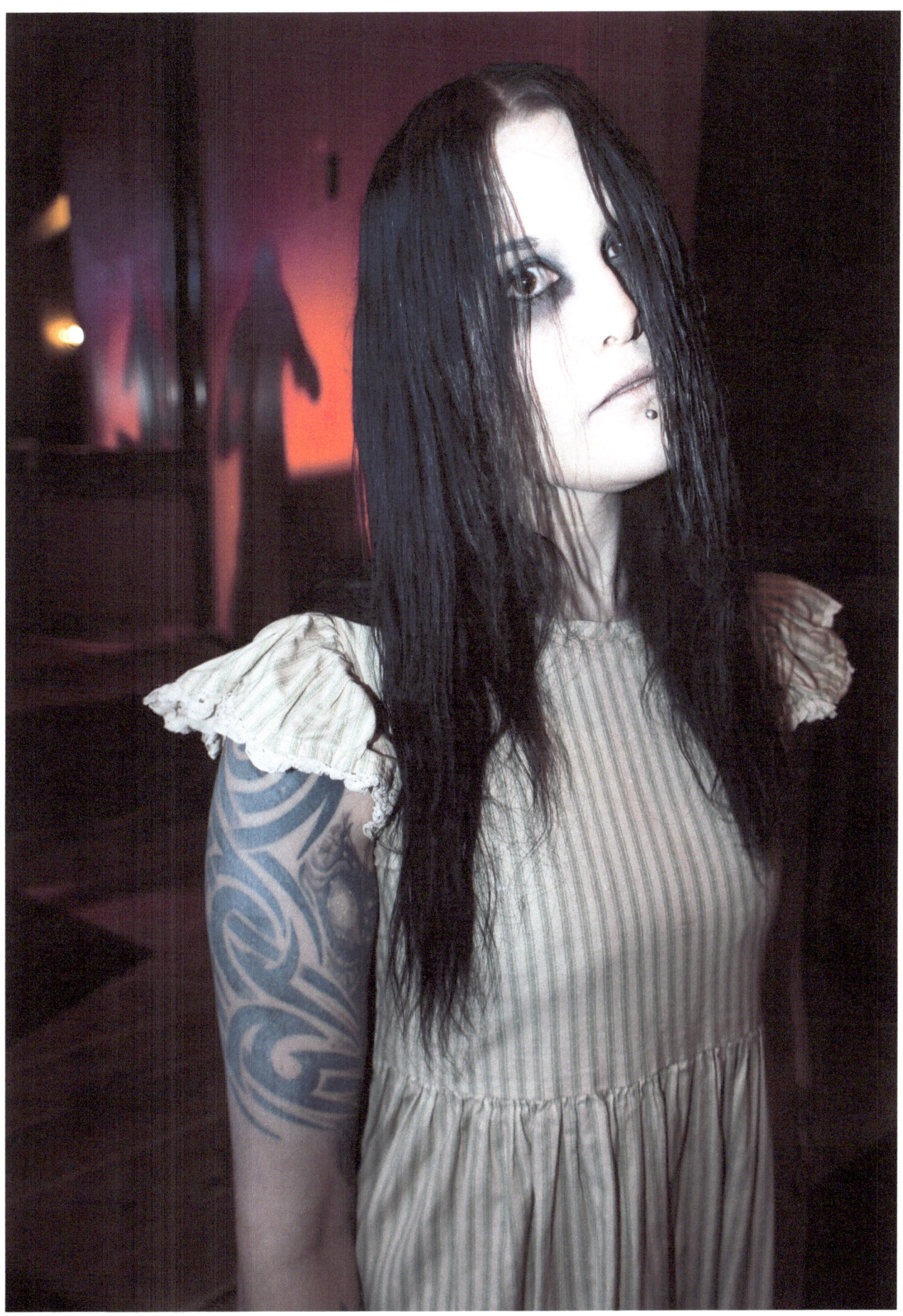

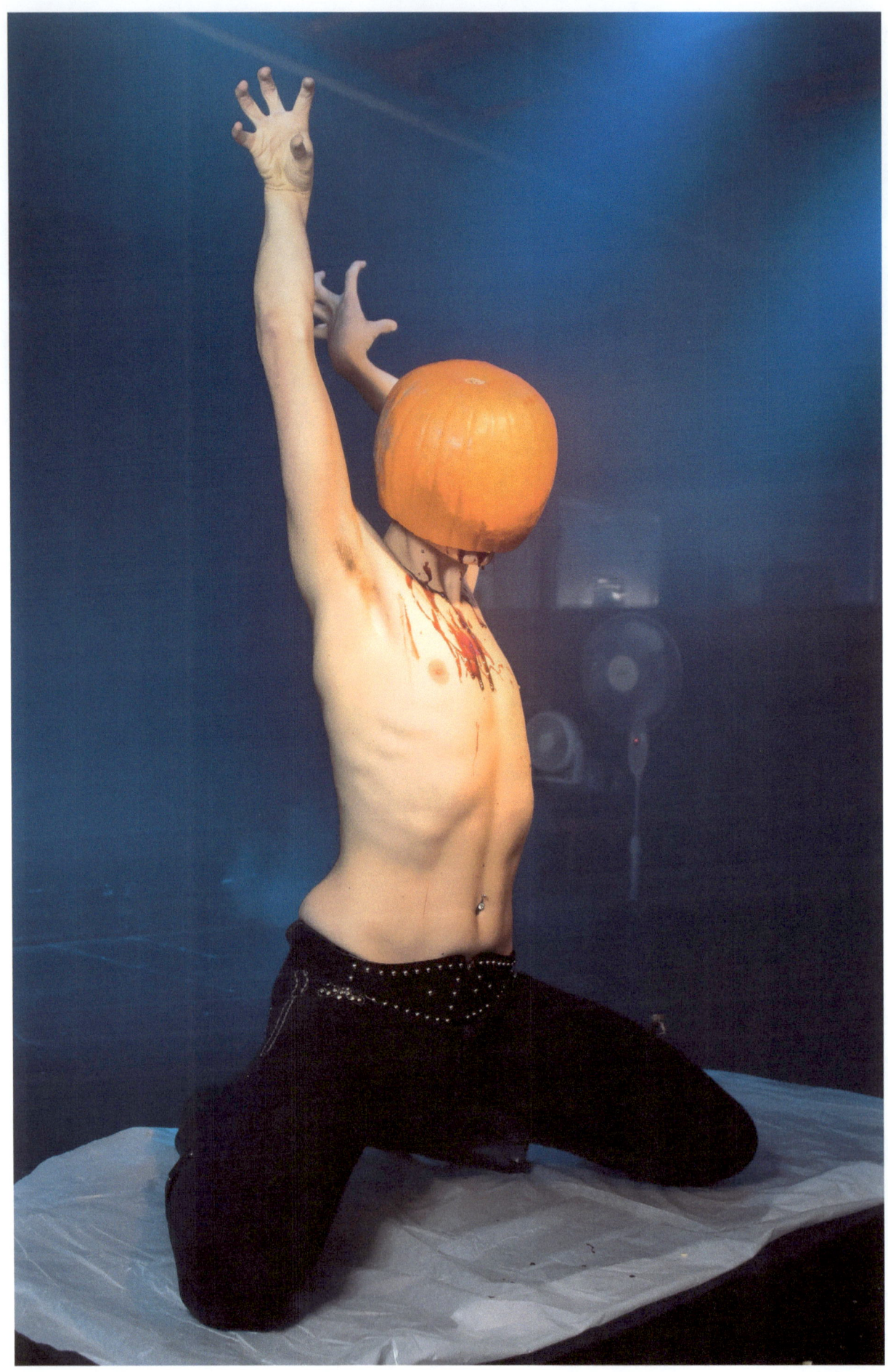

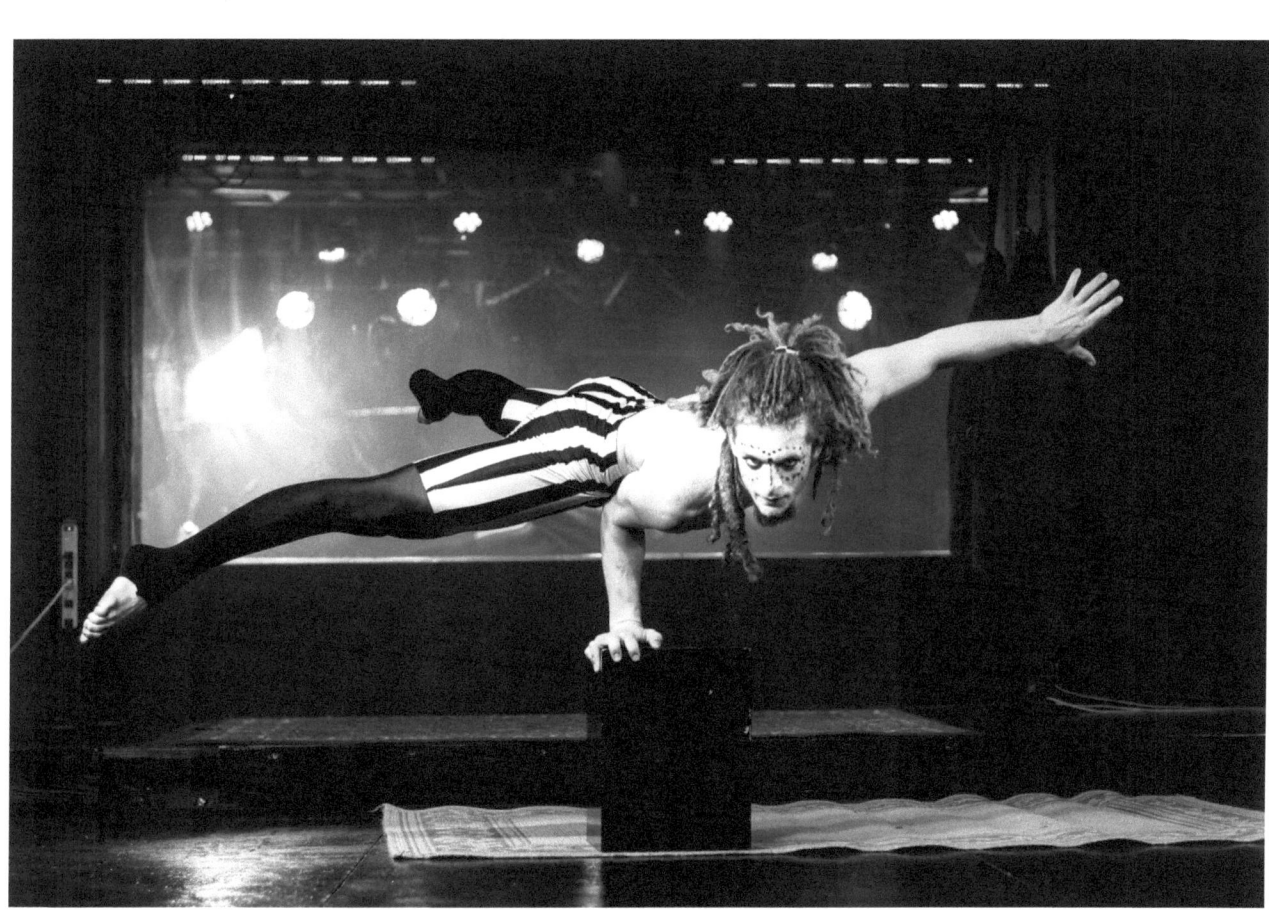

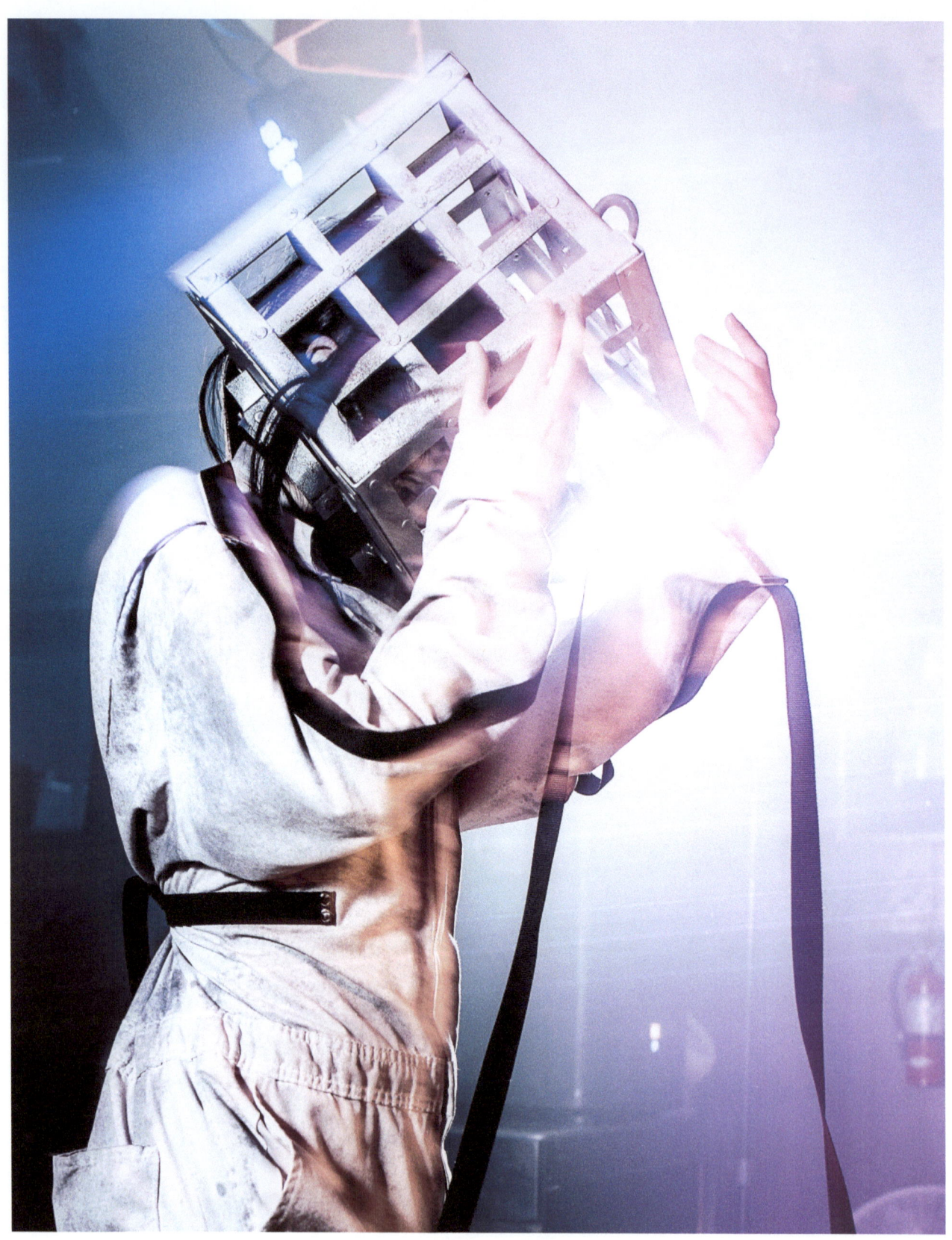

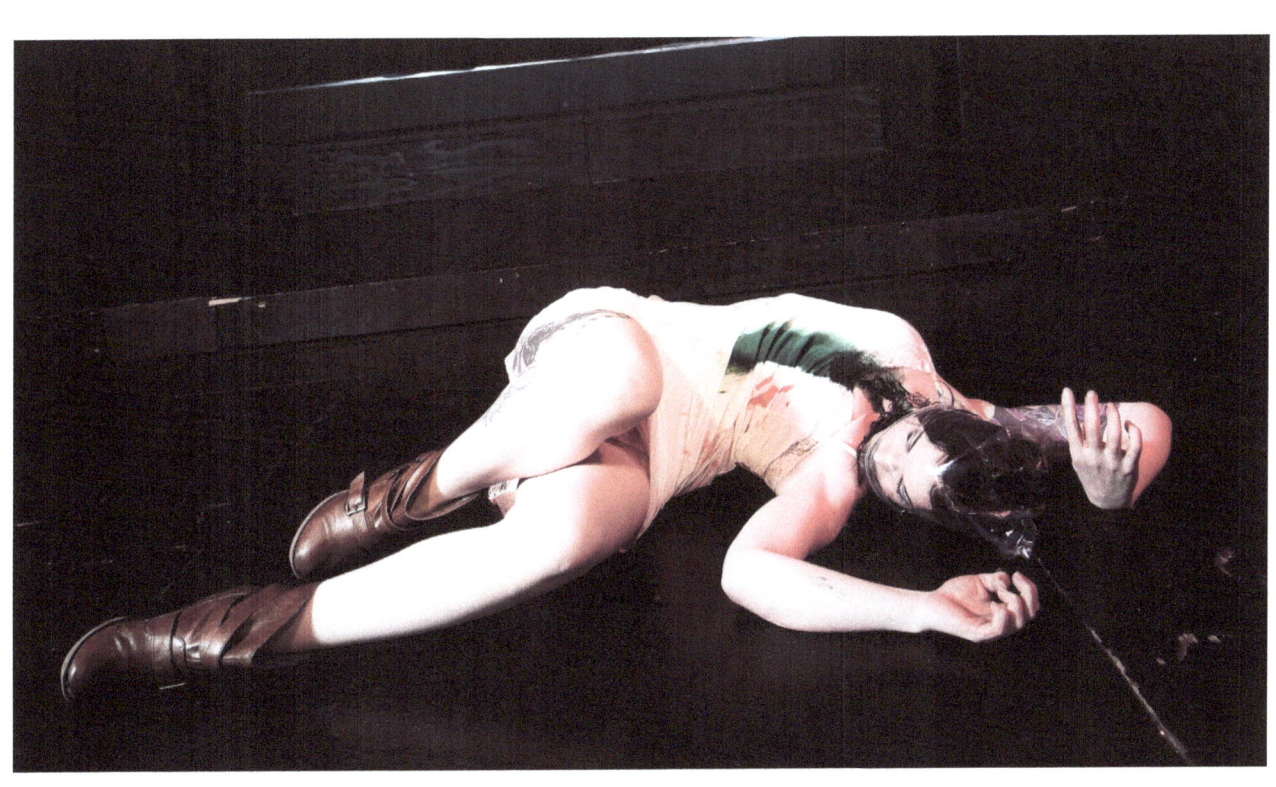

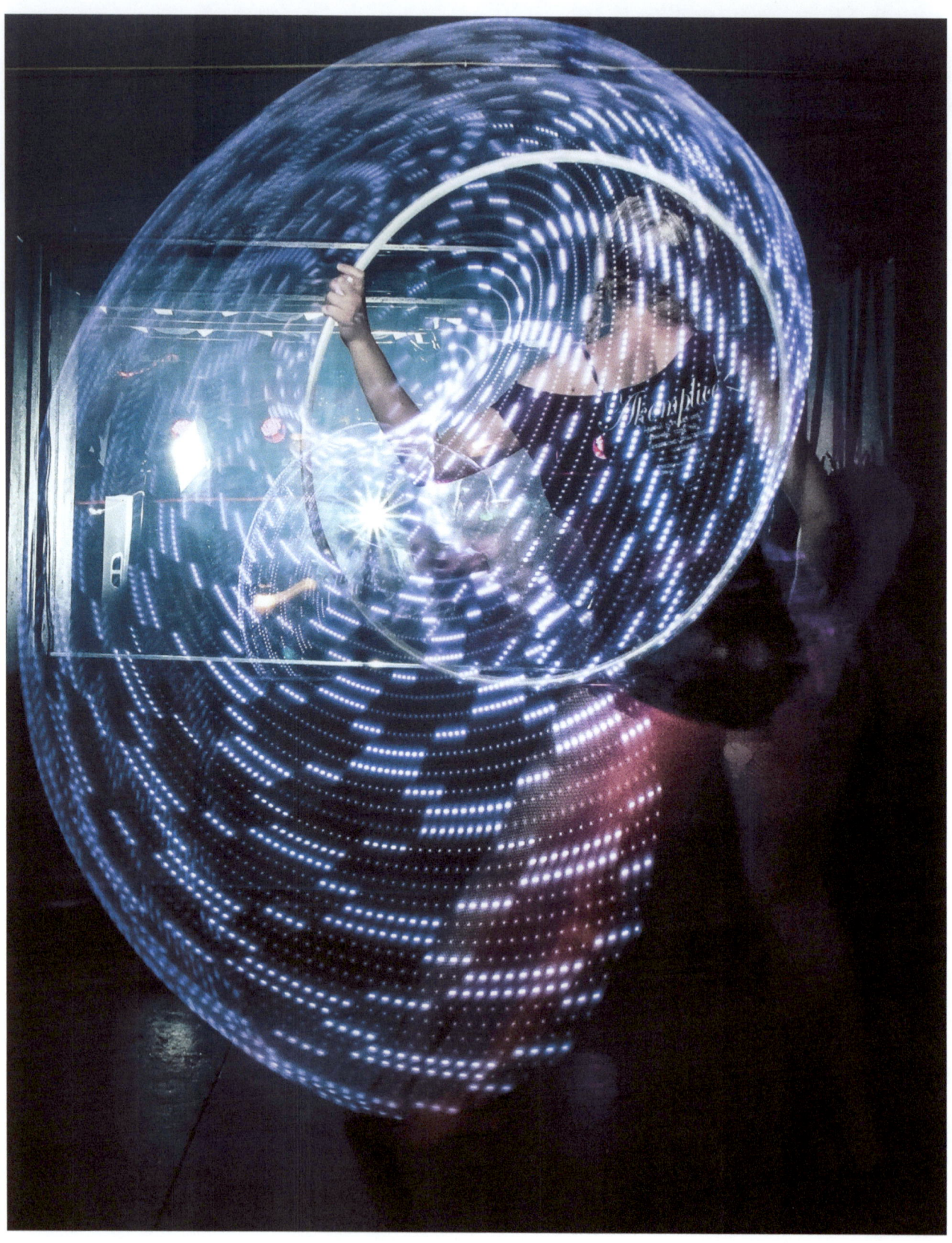

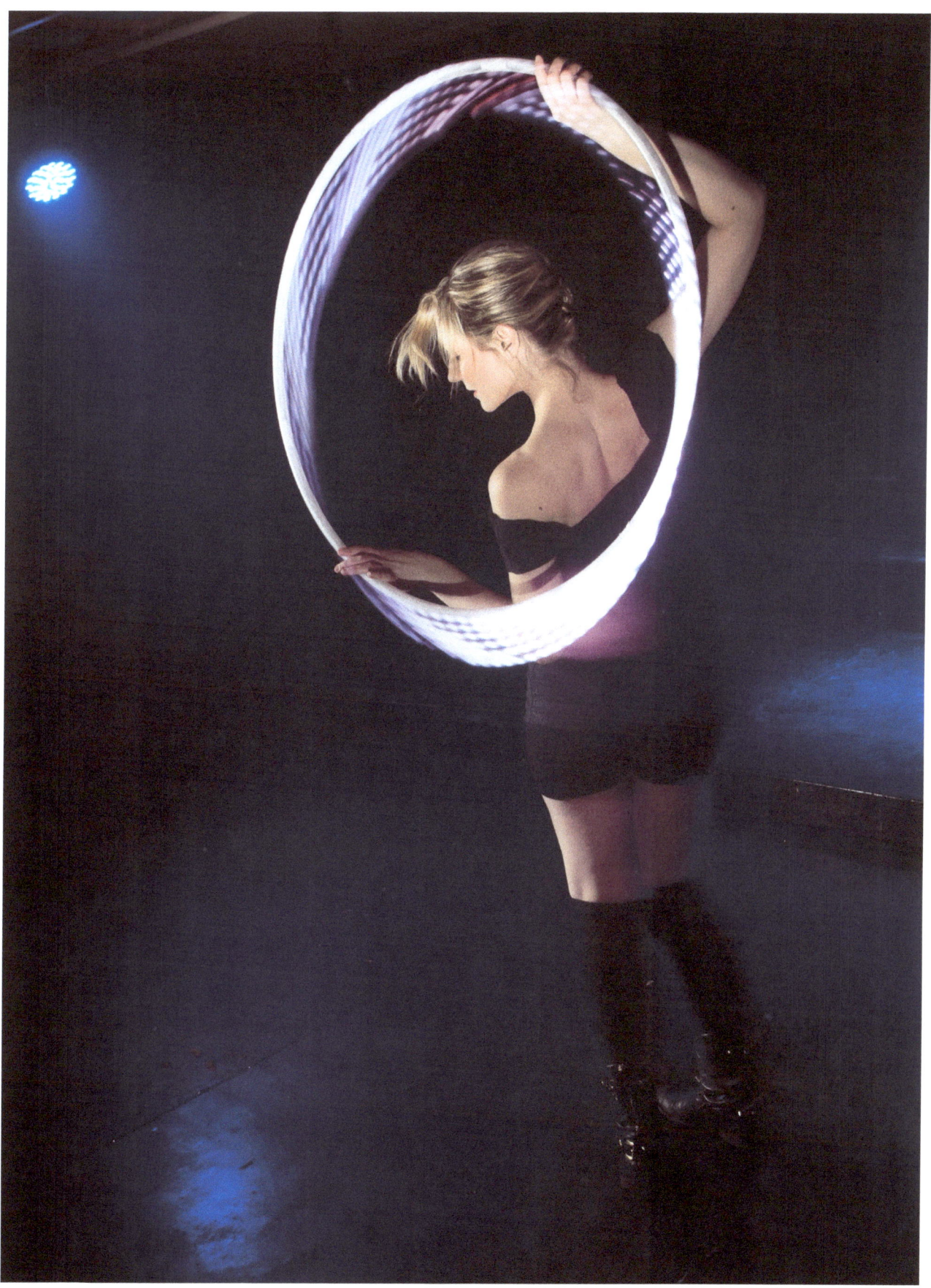

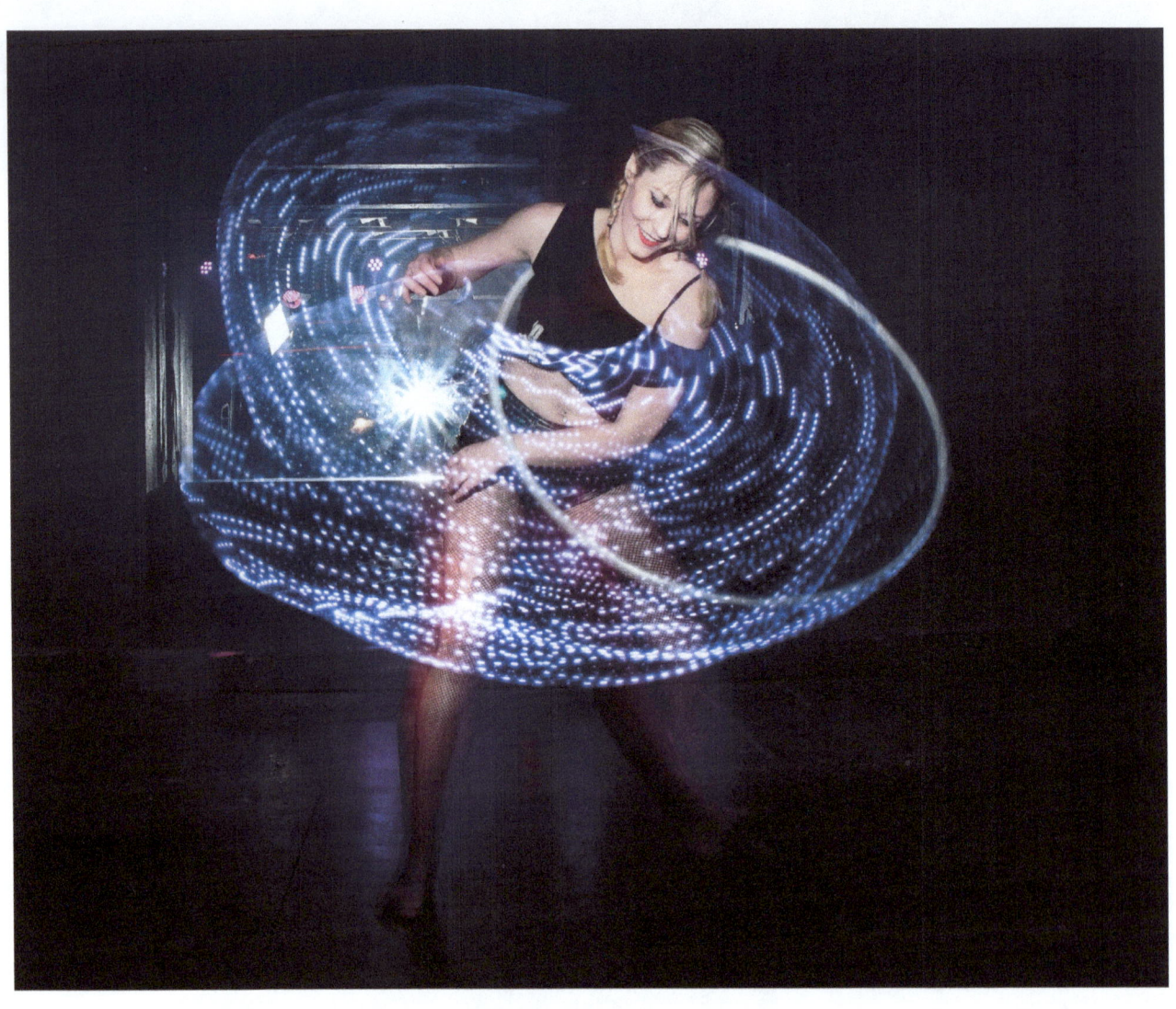

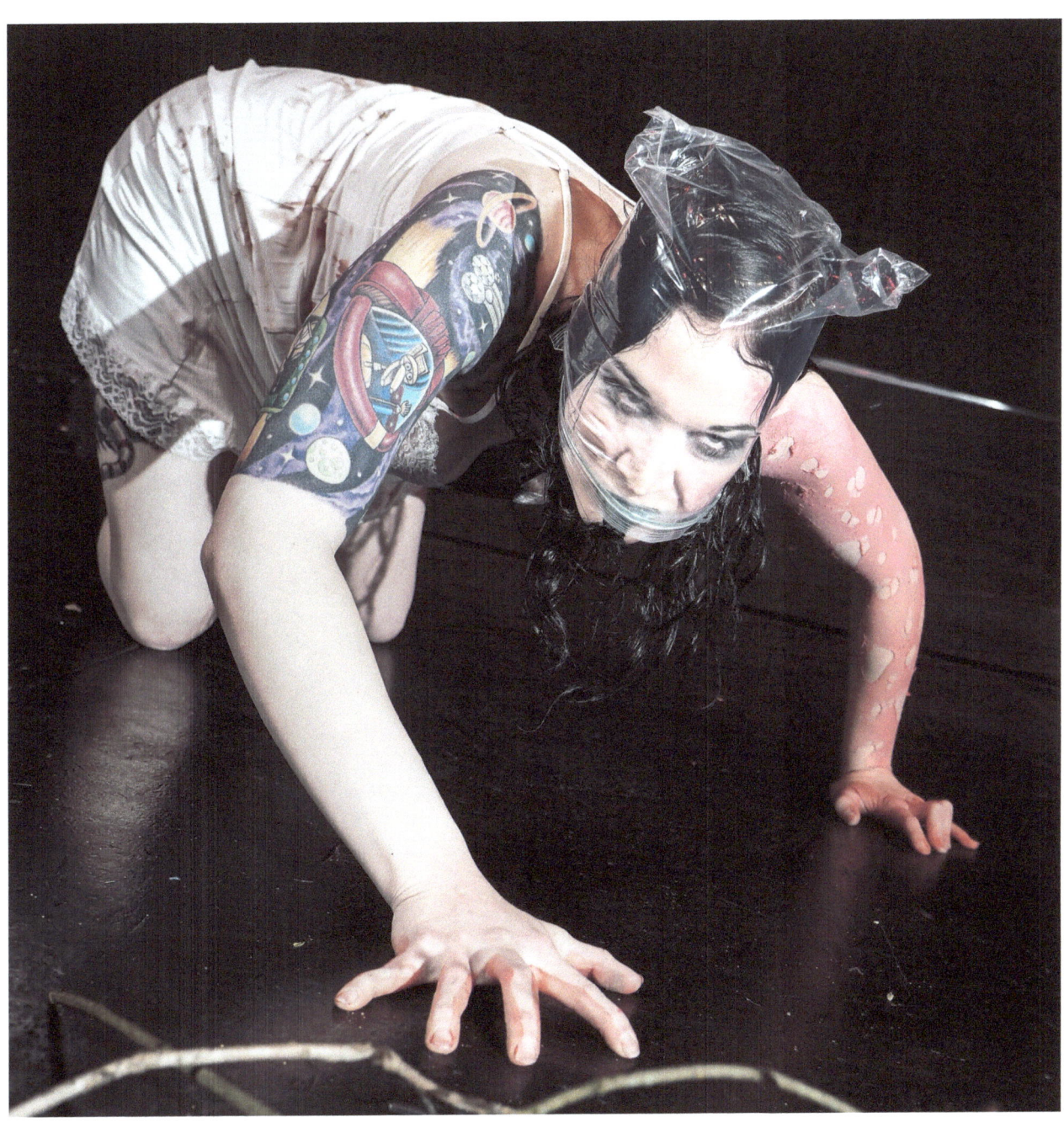

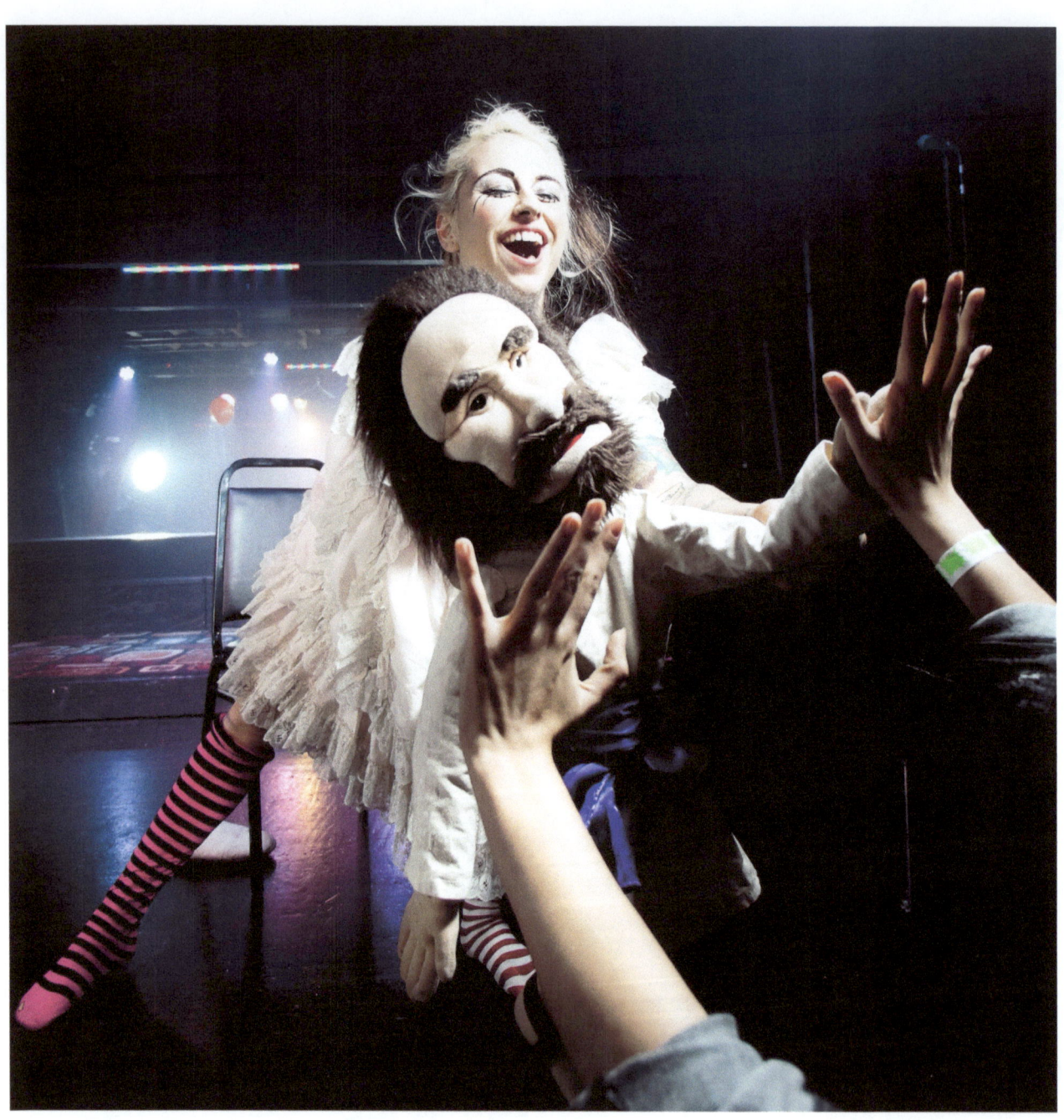

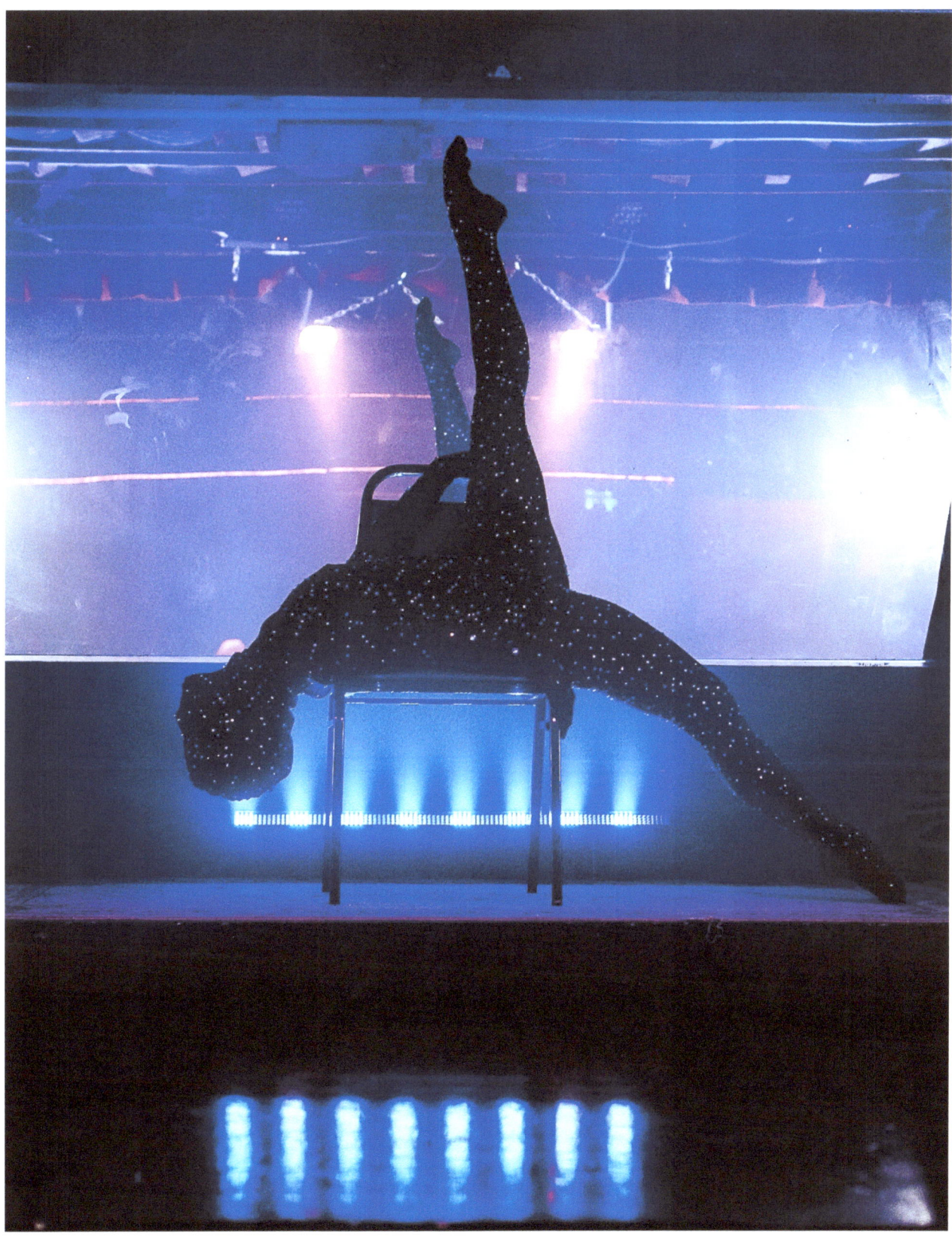

Performers by page

1 - Nik Sin and Gothique
2 - Meg Russel
3 - Valentine Vex
4 - Angie Ziederman
5 - Angie Ziederman
6 - Soren High
7 - Lyric Allure
8 - Surreal de Sade
9 - Zelah Pandemonium
10 - Surka Noelle
11 - Surka Noelle
12 - Soren High
13 - Jon Dutch
14 - Jared Elliot, Alice Faeland
15 - Surreal de Sade
16 - Surreal de Sade
17 - Karlie Lever du Soleil
18 - Shell Bell
19 - Jared Elliot, Zelah Pandemonium
20 - Layne Fawkes
21 - Dr Jay
22 - Fleur de Sel
23 - Russell Bruner
24 - Gothique (Lisa Rife)
25 - Nik Sin
26 - Layne Fawkes
27 - Rummy Rose
28 - Miss Spooky
29 - Nik Sin
30 - Zenith Spins
31 - Sofia Flash
32 - Aaron Schallock
33 - Isaiah Esquire, Johnny Nuriel
34 - Sofia Flash
35 - Alizaire
36 - Bridgetown Revue
37 - Theo Polidori
38 - Aaron Schallock
39 - Gothique (Lisa Rife)
40 - Johnny Nuriel
41 - Josia
42 - Layne Fawkes
43 - Layne Fawkes
44 - Shell Bell
45 - Shell Bell
46 - Shell Bell
47 - Layne Fawkes
48 - Ivizia
49 - DeeDee Luxe

Photography by Tom Good
Edited by Cristina Coppinger